BY IRA HIRSCHMANN

RED
STAR
OVER
BETHLEHEM

RUSSIA DRIVES
TO CAPTURE
THE MIDDLE EAST

BY IRA HIRSCHMANN

SIMON AND SCHUSTER
NEW YORK

First printing

SBN 671-20849-7
Library of Congress Catalog Card Number: 73-139629
Designed by Jack Jaget
Manufactured in the United States of America
By The Book Press Inc., Brattleboro, Vt.

To two lifelong friends—

JOAN   EDITH   STURMAN

whose inspiration never faltered

and

LEO   ROBIN

who titled the book

I owe a deep debt
of gratitude
to
HUGH ORGEL
for his faithful and
invaluable collaboration

CONTENTS

RUSSIA *CONSOLIDATES* HER POSITION 117

RUSSIA *CHALLENGES* THE UNITED STATES 175

PROLOGUE:
REUNION
IN GAZA

Twenty-five years had passed since I had last seen my "children" on a pier in Istanbul. They were then being aroused by Turkish police to march in single file to trains to carry them through Syria to the relatively safe harbor of British-controlled Palestine. I can still see their spindly arms and legs suddenly emerging from the bundles they were clutching—their last possessions. When the train pulled out, the strains of "Hatikwah" (Hope), the national anthem of Israel, surged up from their hearts, emptying out their gratitude.

It was on a battlefield near Gaza two and a half decades later, where I had unexpectedly caught up with the "children," now soldiers in the active reserve of an army of the State of Israel.

As I looked into their eyes and met their clear and steady gaze, the memory of their emaciated bodies and the vacant stares quickly melted away. Tall and strong—shoulders straight, heads up, marching with a firm stance, they were returning from the Sinai battle not in the spirit of "conquerors" but as men and women who had helped secure their State.

The battlefields were still smoldering a few days after the Six-Day War of June 1967 when I arrived in Israel to make a report for the U.S. Department of State to try to find a new approach to the tangled refugee problem in the Gaza Strip and western Jordan, now that the area had come under Israeli occupation. My first visit was to the home of Evan Wilson, the U.S. consul general in Jerusalem, around the corner from the King David Hotel. His house showed the scars of having been hit by shrapnel.

Wilson, a former associate when I was an American envoy during World War II in the American Embassy in Ankara, Turkey, gave me a blow-by-blow story of the war that had exploded in Jerusalem. The urgent pleas of American diplomats to King Hussein to keep his pledge to the U.S. Government to remain neutral had proved futile. At the last moment the king jumped to the side of Egypt's President Nasser. Hussein's excuse was that his life had been threatened: he had to submit his army to Nasser and accept an Egyptian general's overall command. The little king now complained that "It was the worst mistake of my life."

The Israeli high command arranged for me to be driven into the war areas. By appointment, an Israeli army car picked me up at 6 A.M. at my hotel in Tel Aviv. To my astonishment, the middle-aged driver could hardly lift one leg, which was encased in a heavy cast. He explained to me that two days before, in the battle of Jerusalem, a bullet had splintered the leg, but he now managed to use his right foot to control the car's accelerator. As I entered the car rather gingerly, I found two Israelis in full uniform with guns cocked ready for instant action sitting upright in the back. Danger still lurked from the explosives in the battlefields and occasional snipers' bullets.

The first stop was Gaza. It was a ghost town. The shops and windows on the main street were almost hermetically sealed. Large white rags of assorted shapes and sizes hung out of the windows like waving phantoms—unmistakable Arab response to the advancing Israeli army's broadcast: "If you want to stay alive, put out a white flag." The high command had set up an emergency headquarters in the city— soldiers were going from house to house to clean up the last vestiges of resistance and to receive the returning army from the Sinai desert. At the commanding officer's headquarters, I stopped to talk to some of the young Israeli soldiers. In a small alleyway, I came across a stretched-out, relaxed soldier on the pavement, reading a book in Hebrew. A small radio next to him was playing a piece softly which I recognized as the Schubert Impromptu in C. The setting could not have been more incongruous.

As I talked with some of the returning Israeli soldiers, I was startled to learn that most of them had been among the refugees who, at the eleventh hour in 1944, had been carried from the Balkans across the Black Sea and the Bosporus to safety. Teddy Kolleck, now mayor of Jerusalem, and his irrepressible young "boys" from Palestine had at that time helped me assemble an armada of leaky little boats that brought thousands of stranded Jewish children into Istanbul. I had "bought" these children, considered expendable, from Turkish pirates at the bargain-basement rate of $300 a head.

The reunion in Gaza brought back a flood of other memories of hair-raising episodes with Balkan intrigue and Turkish espionage. Among the most bizarre was the special mission on which President Roosevelt had dispatched me in 1944 to represent the United States in the cynical offer made by Adolf Eichmann to exchange "trucks for Jews."

Then a flashback to the 1930's in New York when the news of the massacres in Germany began to seep through. My efforts to arouse Americans, including Jewish leaders, to the plight of thousands of human beings being slaughtered for the reason of their birth was met almost universally with a cool indifference. It seemed unconscionable to me that while blood increasingly spilled from millions of men, women, and children in Central Europe, an unconcerned world, together with its political and religious leaders, remained deaf to their cries. As the slaughter increased, a few isolated attempts by messengers of mercy were made to break through the deathtraps in time to rescue what were by now the remnants of a whole people.

It became my fate to be cast in the strange role of such a messenger. I first sought to call the massacre to the attention of the American public by initiating a boycott of German goods throughout the nation. I managed to succeed in blocking the appointment of Wilhelm Furtwängler, who had accepted from Hermann Goering the post of deputy president of *Musikkammer* of the Third Reich and who was offered the permanent conductorship of the New York Philharmonic Orchestra to succeed Arturo Toscanini, who had defied Hitler's ally, Mussolini. But I soon learned that unofficial gestures were not enough: this was a crisis without precedent that demanded the full weight and prestige of the U.S. Government to be brought to bear on the perpetrators of these genocidal crimes. My exertions for a means of rescue then took priority over my busy life as a department-store executive. A search for peace in the Middle East has since had a first claim on my time.

For months I knocked on the doors of the Department of State in Washington, but to no avail. In 1938, Supreme Court Justice Felix Frankfurter proposed my name as an American delegate to the abortive refugee conference in Evian-les-Bains, France. From there I journeyed to Vienna to witness the *Anschluss* and Austrian anti-Semitism at its most virulent. Through representatives in the United States of the underground in Palestine I was told that rescue operations might be possible from the Balkans through Turkey, which was "neutral" in the war. I urged my friends in the White House to secure permission for me to go to Turkey, and in January 1944 received an appointment as an envoy in Turkey of President Roosevelt to represent the War Refugee Board, comprised of Secretaries of State, the Treasury, and War (Cordell Hull, Henry Morgenthau, Jr., and Henry L. Stimson).

After the founding of Israel in 1948, I made numerous trips to Europe and the Arab capitals as well as to Israel; some were missions under Department of State and United Nations auspices where, visiting the Arab capitals of Damascus, Cairo, Beirut, and Amman. I conferred with Arab leaders, including a secret visit with President Nasser in an unrelenting search for peace, which the Arab people and the Israelis both deserve and will some day have.

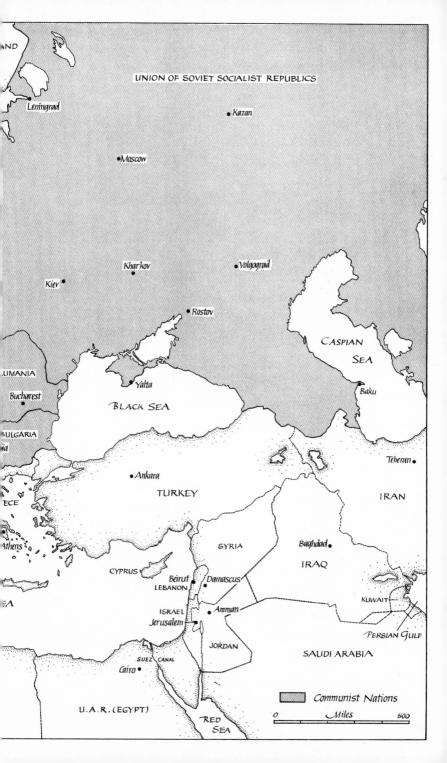

EURASIA

ICELAND

ATLANTIC OCEAN

BARENTS SEA

NORWAY

UNITED KINGDOM

EIRE

FINLAND

DEN. SWEDEN

NETH.

GERMANY W. E.

BELG.

POLAND

UNION OF SOVI

Moscow

Kazan

RUSSIA

AUSTRIA

CZECH.

FRANCE

HUNGARY

PORTUGAL

RUMANIA

SPAIN

YUGOSLAVIA

ITALY

ALB. BULG.

ARAL SEA

CASPIAN SEA

BLACK SEA

MEDITERRANEAN SEA

Tashkent

MOROCCO

GREECE

TURKEY

TUNISIA

SYRIA

ALGERIA

LEBANON

ISRAEL

IRAQ

Teheran

IRAN

Kabu

AFGHANISTAN

JORDAN

KUWAIT

PAKIST

LIBYA

U.A.R. (EGYPT)

Riyadh

Karachi

SAUDI ARABIA

OMAN

ARABIAN SEA

RED SEA

YEMEN

ADEN

SUDAN

AFRICA

INDIA

palacios

Communist Nations

RUSSIA
AIMS
FOR THE
MIDDLE
EAST

To Mr Hutchman
with the best wishes
and highest regards

Jamal Abdul

I

MY
MEETING
WITH
NASSER

Gamal Abdel Nasser sat facing me. His fanatical brown eyes seemed to drill through me as he leaned his swarthy face toward me, took a long puff on his cigarette, and in measured English said: "If I can't get major arms from the Americans, I will get them from the Russians." It was August 1955, and the thermometer in Cairo registered 110 degrees. A decade and a half later the political thermometer was to reach boiling point.

We were in the living room of the Egyptian leader's modest villa outside Heliopolis, a suburb of Cairo. The other person present was Abdul Kader Hatem, the Egyptian minister of information, a member of the officers' group which had staged the successful coup against King Farouk in 1952. By appointment, Hatem had escorted me from the Semiramis Hotel facing the Nile in Cairo into a funereal-looking limousine whose black blinds were slammed tight as I entered the car and remained shut throughout the full hour's ride to Nasser's home. The purpose of the drawn blinds was to keep the meeting in utmost secrecy, but as the car snaked through Cairo's crowded streets and the suburbs to Nasser's home, I felt like a "prisoner" in a Kafka novel.

The secret meeting that had been arranged outside American diplomatic channels ended in a relaxed climate, and Nasser sent me back to the hotel with an implied promise to keep an open door for a moratorium in the shooting across the borders, along with his photograph bearing a friendly inscription to me. It was informally agreed that he would accept me as a private liaison between him and the Israeli leaders as long as there was no "leak." (Hatem and I had agreed in advance that if any of the newsmen or the myriad spies who infested Cairo got wind of private talks between Israel's most virulent enemy and an American of Jewish faith categorical denials would be made by both sides.)

How did I, a former American diplomatic envoy prominently identified with the rescue of refugees from Hitler through Turkey into Palestine, manage to arrive at a face-to-face confrontation with the leader of the Arabs at a moment when his armies were poised for a "second round" of war with Israel? Nasser had succeeded in uniting Arab military forces under his guidance and had forged a "ring of steel" around the besieged people of Israel, faced with a tightening of the ring by the concerted armies of the Arabs and the terror raids by Fedayeen from Gaza, Jordan, and Syria. It was another hour of peril for the people of Israel. I had been given an informal assignment to see what could be done with the Egyptian leader in establishing a moratorium in the border strife, a formula that I had worked out with George V. Allen, Assistant Secretary of State and head of the Middle East desk there. But Nasser was then in no mood to deal with the United States in a spirit of conciliation. He had feuded with the U.S. Ambassador, Henry A. Byroade, and as a result relations between the Egyptian and the U.S. governments had been ruptured. Assistant Secretary Allen hoped that a meeting between Nasser and an American diplomat not formally connected with our embassy in Cairo might help to re-establish relations between the two countries at a critical hour.

"Why do you need major arms if your policy is peace in the area?" I asked the Egyptian leader.

"I must defend my people from the Israelis" was his quick reply.

The twenty minutes that had been allotted for our meeting had already stretched beyond an hour. The only interruption in the dimly lit room was the shadowlike appearance of a Nubian servant, clad in a white gown that reached to the ground, who served a soft sarsaparilla-flavored beverage that I drank with some hesitation.

Again and again I had steered the dialogue away from Nasser's diatribe against Israel, the issue of the border strife.

"I have lost confidence in the United States and Great Britain," he continued, however.

"And Russia?" I interrupted.

He went on: "Eisenhower and Dulles are stalling on major arms. I cannot wait any longer. I will be obliged to turn to the East."

At that moment, Nasser's deputies were already in active negotiation with Kremlin agents for the purchase of a major arsenal of arms. On May 18, 1955, at a reception of the Sudan embassy in Cairo, Nasser broached the subject of the arms purchase to the Russian Ambassador, Daniel S. Golod, and within three days Nikita Khrushchev consented to an agreement, but stipulated that the deal should be made with Czechoslovakia. When I arrived in Cairo in July, it was not known to Washington that papers were ready for signature in Prague for the purchase of major arms. Nasser was not bluffing. On September 27 he disclosed the deal, a breakthrough that was to inject Russia for the first time as an active military and political force in the heart of the Middle East, starting a chain reaction that is today convulsing the area and threatening a worldwide conflict.

After my meeting with Nasser I flew to Israel via Cyprus to meet with Prime Minister Moshe Sharett and David Ben-Gurion, the minister of defense, who still pulled the strings of power—he was to return to the premiership within the year.

Ben-Gurion expressed astonishment that Nasser had met with me and had talked so frankly, considering my Jewish faith and background. I told him that my meeting had been arranged through subterranean channels and that Nasser's agents had checked me and followed my every movement in Cairo for a whole week before he saw me at his home.

Ben-Gurion listened to my recital of the colloquy with Nasser with a somewhat distracted air. "Nasser will not long remain on the horse," he summed up cavalierly. Emphatically, but to no effect, I disagreed and insisted that my observations on the scene in Egypt indicated conclusively that Nasser was there to stay for a long pull.

Sharett, on the other hand, was quick to sense that my personal liaison with the Egyptian leader might help to arrest the deteriorating relations between the two countries. "We must grasp at the tenderest thread for peace," he said. Sharett called a special cabinet meeting, after which he begged me to return to Cairo with specific proposals to Nasser.

My itinerary called for me to move on to Turkey, where I was to meet Prime Minister Adnan Menderes, but I unhesitatingly agreed to return to Cairo to deliver the secret Israeli proposals to Nasser.

After conferring with our American ambassador, Edward B. Lawson, in Tel Aviv and getting clearance from Washington, I made plans to return to Cairo. I was obliged to stop over in Cyprus, where I ran into a bureaucratic mare's nest. The youthful Egyptian consul general in Nicosia had no word of my schedule to proceed to Cairo. And as my passport contained a stamp of an enemy country (Israel), he refused to validate my visa to Egypt. After a few difficult days in Nicosia arguing with the Egyptian consul general (our American consul general was out of the country), I finally hit on the expedient of showing him the photograph that Nasser had given me with his signed inscription. This almost bowled over the young consul general, and I flew off to breathe again the sweltering 110-degree fetid odor of Cairo. But Indian Prime Minister Nehru was making a state visit to his friend Nasser at that moment, and I could not transmit Sharett's proposal in person. I finally agreed to have it transmitted through Abdul Kadar Hatem, Nasser's information chief.

On my return to Washington to make my report to George V. Allen in the Department of State, he ruefully observed: "Well, Ira, you made history. You're the only man who has ever seen Nasser and Ben-Gurion on the same day." Small solace, indeed, for a mission born of the passion for peace shared by the people of both Egypt and Israel.

Nasser made good on two threats he had announced to me in his living room. He had hinted that Nūri Said, the Iraqi prime minister, would be eliminated. And indeed, in a bloody coup on July 14, 1958, Nūri Said was murdered by a mob, and his body was dragged through the streets of Baghdad. Nasser also got his arms from the Soviet bloc. He furthermore nationalized the Suez Canal on July 26, 1956, a step which led, three months later, to the first Suez War in 1956, now a blighted page in the history books. Washington had steered itself into the unthinkable position of siding with Moscow against London and Paris. Under the guidance of Secretary of State John Foster Dulles, England and France were forced from the Suez, and Israel had to retreat from Sinai as the result of one of the most cynical and serious blunders in American diplomacy. With one stroke, Eisenhower and Dulles eliminated England and France as powers in the Middle East and put Nasser, who had been unhorsed, back in the saddle, and allowed Russia to emerge as the major power in the Middle East, thus setting the stage for the June 1967 war.

But the purpose of this book is not to review the frustrations involved in any one well-meaning effort at mediation in an area that has become increasingly combustible. I was present when Nasser invited the Soviets into Egypt with an exchange of his cotton crop for Czech and Russian arms. I can pinpoint the events almost to the hour which led one man to spring open a door at which the Russians had knocked for 300 years, permitting them to inject themselves inside Egypt and the Middle East as the military arbiters, the decisive force for war or peace in the area.

Ever since the days of Catherine the Great, this had been Russia's dream, a dream which if realized would collide with the policies of London and Paris.

It was the firm action of the British and French in the nineteenth century against the threat of the Russian take-over of the Ottoman Empire, the controlling but declining power in the Middle East, which thwarted Russia's aims. Even today, in this era of supersonic aircraft and intercontinental missiles, the Middle East is of major pivotal importance in the struggle for world balance of power, an importance possibly even greater than that of Vietnam in southeastern Asia. Since the exit of the British from the Middle East at the end of World War II, the Soviet Union has worked, first stealthily and then steadily, to move into the power vacuum and achieve their historic aim of controlling the area.

At stake are not merely United States economic interests, since World War II represented by prodigious investments in oil. Of even greater importance is the free world's need to safeguard this turnstile among three continents. It was the vacillating policy of the United States in the 1950's that let down the bars for Russian entry into the area through Egypt where, twenty years later, they are now poised to spring into aerial military action against Israel. It is this tiny nation which is blocking their take-over of Suez and preventing further consolidation of Russia's hold on the Middle East. Without a secure Israel, Russia could outflank the U.S. Sixth Fleet guarding the southern borders of the

Mediterranean members of the Western allies and could move into the Persian Gulf and the Indian Ocean. Ironically, oil interests in the United States appear blind to the fact that Israel is blocking the Soviet drive to take over the Saudi Arabian oil fields.

Such a firm stance does not in any sense mean a commitment of American soldiers to the area. Israel has demonstrated its capacity to do its own fighting and to stand up in the face of Russian threats, provided it receives from us essential economic and military support. But continued vacillation in the face of Russian advances in the vital Middle East may hasten an East-West confrontation under circumstances that could be decidedly more devastating to the United States and all Western interests than that which they are today suffering in southeastern Asia.

Nasser's fateful decision to invite the Russians to entrench themselves at the gateway between East and West signaled a hurricane of events in history, the violence of which we are only beginning to witness in the Middle East eruption. For behind the façade of an Egyptian army is the Soviet Union's third multibillion-dollar arsenal with its 10,000 military "advisors," air-force generals, pilots, and missile operators alongside the Suez Canal as the real adversary of peace in the Middle East.

Looking back at the egocentric temperament and unbridled drive that revealed itself in the personality of the late Egyptian leader during the long talk in his home, I can now understand why I was in a position throughout the years to interpret some of the reckless exploits with which he brought Egypt to the verge of economic collapse, as well as his motives for providing an open door to the Russians.

Nasser spoke to me feelingly of his awareness of the critical need for reforms to uplift his people. This immense task which faced him from within offered too little of the spectacular to satisfy his insatiable appetite for glory and prestige. Instead, he turned to external dramatic adventures in Syria, Yemen and Israel, none of which his country could afford and all of which ended in disaster.

In the American embassy in Damascus in 1960, it was not difficult for me to foresee that the "marriage" which Nasser had forced upon the Syrian leaders was bound to break up, as it did six months later. The 70,000 troops which Nasser had committed to a military adventure in Yemen aimed at the underbelly of Saudi Arabia was a "wild" long shot doomed to failure from the start. The same held true when he swallowed his own propaganda in May 1967 and exposed his army to disastrous defeat at the hands of the Israelis.

II

THE SECRET
BEHIND THE
SIX-DAY WAR

The lightning triumph of the Israelis in June 1967 opened up what seemed at the time myriad possibilities for the long-sought peace in the Middle East. The infested Arab refugee camps in the Gaza Strip and in Jordan west of the Jordan River were opened for the first time to the Israelis for examination of their true numbers and possible employment.

I had visited the Arab refugee camps on several studies under U.S. Department of State and United Nations auspices since 1960. Immediately following the end of the Six-Day War on June 11, 1967, the Department of State authorized me to leave at once for Israel to make a new study and evaluation, now that the areas had been occupied by Israel.

At this time, while working in the American embassy in Tel Aviv, I learned of the momentous events that had led to the Six-Day War, secrets that have baffled the political analysts and confused the Middle East experts. To this date, the truth has never been revealed or told in concise form. It is an almost unbelievable tale: the Russians wrote the script; Syria, Egypt, and Israel were to play their assigned parts to fit a scenario, with the Kremlin hiding safely in the wings.

The play fell apart when the Syrians, Egyptians, and Israelis refused to follow the Russian script. In fact, each rewrote his own part in characteristic style. For the Israelis, no final written script was prepared. Their part in the Russian plan was not to react to Arab lines of provocation. React they did not. *Act* they did. And after a lightning six-day drama, the curtain went down with a bang, the Egyptians scurrying across the Suez Canal for cover, the Syrians retreating beyond the Golan Heights, and Israel taking the bows. Forced to act, at the peril of her very existence, the Israelis would have preferred, and still prefer, the script of their ancient prophets, which her people have rehearsed for two thousand years—the script of peace.

The Russians counted too heavily on their ability to manipulate their Arab clients and to use their crushing power to intimidate the Israelis by assigning to all of them roles on a slippery political stage on which they were expected to dance to the Kremlin's tune. Moscow's experience with the Arab leaders should have taught them that you cannot buy an Arab, you can only rent him. The Soviets also vastly underestimated the will of the Israelis not to panic, and the powerful military punch they packed.

The story begins in the spring of 1967. The Syrians were spoiling for an assault on Israel, but the Soviet Union was determined to restrain them, fearing loss of control over the leaders in Damascus. Syria occupies a pivotal position in Russia's southern-tier defense line. The Kremlin strategy is to build a *cordon sanitaire* around Russia's borders, using Iraq and Syria for a wall of defense against any possible invasion of Russia from the Middle East countries. They were to leapfrog Turkey, a member of NATO occupying a common border with the Soviet Union, whom the Russians could not control. The defensive role assigned to Iraq and Syria by the Russians differed completely from that intended for Egypt, which was to be a springboard for the Kremlin's Middle East offensive.

Moscow had its hands full in holding its reins tightly on Syria. The people of Syria have long been the most volatile and unstable in the Arab Middle East. It was in the narrow markets and coffeehouses of Damascus that the idea of Arab national independence was debated and came to birth.

In 1965, I was a guest for a week in Damascus of Robert Borden Reams, who was then U.S. minister to Syria. Reams had been chargé of the U.S. embassy in Yugoslavia in 1949, and I had then developed a close friendship with him when I was sent by the Department of State to meet secretly with Marshal Tito in an attempt to determine whether the break with Stalin was real or a political "trick."

In Damascus, I was able to share with Reams his shrewd political analysis and appraisal on the scene of the fermenting Syrian politics. It was clear that the Syrians, then allied with Egypt under Nasser's UAR, would soon break away from that marriage of convenience. The hatred of the Syrians for the Egyptians could almost be felt in the air. They referred to the Egyptians as "mongrel" Arabs, not remotely in the same class with the sophisticated Syrians. It was clear from my briefings how unstable the Syrian leaders and politics were and why one Syrian government and regime would follow another in quick succession in a continuing series of revolts and rebellions. The Syrian Ba'ath party which took control in 1960 was quick to show sympathy with the aims of the Soviet Union, and the Kremlin was equally quick to respond. For Syria lies in what is termed in Soviet parlance "close proximity to the borders of the Soviet Union"—a phrase always used when referring to areas of special strategic importance for Soviet defense.

In view of the volatility of the Syrian people and the "close proximity" of Syria (separated from Soviet borders by only a thin wedge of Turkey, Iraq, and Iran) the Soviet's firm policy is to maintain pro-Soviet regimes in power in Damascus. Moscow at this time had every reason to be worried about stability in Damascus. During the last months of 1966 and the first months of 1967 report followed report, and rumor chased rumor about impending governmental changes or revolts in the Syrian capital.

Syria had mastered the established practice in the Arab states of meeting fears of weakness and upsets within by increased barrages of verbal hostility against Israel, with the aim of deflecting local unrest away from local politics. But now words in Syria were accompanied by terrorist activity against Israel, for she had served as a base for the recruitment, training, and equipment of Arab terrorist groups.*

The Syrian terrorist raids against Israel accelerated through the first five months of 1967, leading to civilian Israeli deaths

---

* Not always for use against Israel. During the autumn of 1969 the terrorist groups were used by Syria in an attempt to intimidate Lebanon, a neighboring Arab state. By 1970, the terrorists had taken over control of large areas of southern Lebanon, and the stability of the Beirut government was severely threatened.

in border villages and to a running air battle in which Israeli jets shot down six Syrian Russian-built MIG fighters as well as Israel's retaliation against the military bases from which the terrorists operated. Israel's strong action resulted in growing fears for the stability of the Syrian government and the possible loosening of Soviet control.

The aim of restraining the Syrians was behind the visit of Soviet Premier Kosygin to Cairo in May 1966, when he suggested that Nasser sign a mutual defense pact between Egypt and Syria. But Syria did not comply. In fact, the Syrians pressed the Russians to supply arms to the Syrian-raised terrorist groups to enable them to escalate their raids against Israel. The Russians refused, and the Syrians threatened to go shopping in Peking. At this juncture, even UN Secretary General U Thant became alarmed, going so far as to tell the press that the incidents were "very deplorable" and that the specialized training the Syrians appeared to have received in Syria "menaces the peace of the area." Coming from U Thant, this was strong language indeed when directed against an Arab source.

Moscow's fear of losing control of the weakened regime in Damascus was evidenced by a series of six diplomatic notes that (I learned in Jerusalem) had been presented by the Soviet ambassador to Israel during the eight months prior to the Six-Day War. Each of those notes stressed Russia's interest in Syria and its "close proximity to the borders of the Soviet Union." Each hinted that it was in Israel's best interests not to retaliate against Syrian provocation. Each contained the implied threat that the USSR would ultimately control the whole Middle East area, including Israel, and would be the arbiters of peace or war (a "confession" which cannot be overlooked in the light of the Kremlin's present moves in the region). Dimitri Chouvakhine, the Soviet ambassador to Israel, repeatedly made informal inquiries of Israel's Foreign Ministry officials to ascertain how Israel was reacting to these notes. The Kremlin was becoming increasingly worried at the possible effect on the unstable Syrian regime of the predictable Israeli military answer to terrorist raids from Syria. But this was not the only danger confronting Damascus.

Toward the end of April 1967, the Syrian army newspaper carried a strong atheistic article ridiculing Islam and the Prophet Mohammed. Although the Damascus regime was militaristic and radical, it had till then never dared attack Islam or offend the religious susceptibilities of the religious Moslems. The Islamic leaders rose up, called protest meetings, and harangued the worshipers in the mosques, calling for a firm stand against the "godless communists." One of the chief 'Ulamā' (Islamic theologians) was arrested and his property confiscated, but this led only to increased rioting against the government and more violence in the large cities. The pro-Soviet Syrian government now appeared to be in danger of collapse. If it were to be brought down by religion-incited mobs, an anti-Soviet regime would probably take its place. Russia clearly had to take action.

Moscow's solution was to persuade Nasser to come to the aid of Damascus.

In March, Andrei Gromyko paid an unexpected and secret visit to Egypt. He told Nasser that Moscow could no longer control the hotheads in Syria and restrain their terrorist attacks against Israel. Moscow also could not control Israeli retaliation; the Israelis had firmly rejected all the Soviet diplomatic notes with their implied threats. War appeared inevitable, Gromyko said, and war would lead to the overthrow of the pro-Soviet regime in Syria. He demanded that Egypt act to draw Israeli attention away from Syria and relieve the pressure there by providing a diversion on Israel's southern border with Egypt. He outlined the scenario. Nasser should demand the withdrawal of the United Nations Emergency Force which had been placed along the Egyptian-Israel border in the Sinai, along the Gaza Strip border, and at Sharm e-Sheikh—a strategic point at the entrance to the Gulf of Aqaba, from which Israeli forces had been persuaded to withdraw after the Sinai campaign of 1956. Egypt was furthermore to move its troops into the Sinai, advancing in the general direction of the Israeli border. But Gromyko added a stern warning: don't shoot and don't shout too loudly; the aim and object is not war, but to divert the Israelis from the Syrian border. The Israelis are going through a severe economic crisis, the Soviet foreign minister told Nasser, and probably would not be able to afford an all-out war at present, but no chances should be taken.

The excuse for the movement of Egyptian troops into the Sinai would be reports of the massing of Israeli troops on the Syrian border.

When the "news" of the massed Israeli troops reached the Israeli government in Jerusalem, Premier Levi Eshkol invited all the foreign ambassadors in Israel to take a trip to the area to see for themselves the falseness of the reports. Only Chouvakhine, the Soviet ambassador who had previously been busy checking up on Israeli reactions, refused to take the two-hour car trip to the northern border: it would have been just too embarrassing to have to report back to the Kremlin, which had first manufactured the rumor, that it was completely untrue.

The UN Secretary General also checked up on the reports

of Israeli troops massing on the borders. In his report to the Security Council on May 19, 1967, U Thant wrote:

> The government of Israel very recently assured me that there are no unusual Israel troop concentrations or movements along the Syrian line, that there will be none and that no military action will be initiated by the armed forces of Israel unless such action is first taken by the other side.
>
> Reports from UNTSO observers have confirmed the absence of troop concentrations and significant troop movements on both sides of the line.

Before acting on the UNEF withdrawal demand, Nasser consulted with Nehru and Tito, his "neutralist" Indian and Yugoslavian associates, both of whom had national contingents in the United Nations Emergency Force. Both advised Nasser against making the demand because of the possible danger of war. Soviet pressure for action continued, however; and Nasser finally gave way, but then he departed from the prepared script. He demanded—and U Thant agreed—to immediate withdrawal of UNEF. He moved his troops forward into the Sinai, and he didn't shoot, as he had been ordered not to. Up to this point the Soviet Union's strategy had been successful. But the Kremlin leaders had failed to reckon with Nasser's garrulousness and temperament which got the best of him and led him to take further action not in the scenario. He did shout, and loudly. In addition to demanding the withdrawal of UNEF from the Israel-Sinai border and the Gaza Strip, he also demanded and got the UN Secretary General's agreement to the withdrawal of UNEF from Sharm e-Sheikh. Sensing the rising tide of enthusiasm within the Arab world and taunted by the other Arab states to close the Straits of Tiran at the entrance of the Gulf of Aqaba, Nasser lost his head. On May 24 he announced the blockade of the straits against Israeli shipping to and from Israel.

Moscow knew full well that this action would be regarded by the Israelis as a *casus belli* and in fact legitimate cause for action by the United States and the Western powers which had guaranteed freedom of passage through this international waterway at the time of Israel's withdrawal from the Straits of Tiran in 1956. Nasser now reversed this 1956 decision. Moscow was furious: it saw the crisis getting out of control, but it was too late. Israel and Egypt were on a collision course. Within two weeks the war had broken out, and within another week it was over, with Israeli troops standing firm along the Suez Canal, the Jordan River, and within thirty miles of Damascus.

There are two interesting sidelights to this scenario: Nasser covered up the negotiations he had had with Gromyko in March by stating in his "abdication speech" right after his colossal defeat in the June war (he had previously arranged for a spontaneous street demonstration to demand the withdrawal of his resignation) that the news of the alleged massing of Israeli troops had been given in Moscow to a visiting delegation of Egyptian parliamentarians—an unusual channel for the transmission of diplomatic advice of this importance.

Another sidelight reveals how the Russians had used their Middle Eastern allies in the days before the war to put unrelenting pressure on Israel. The pro-Soviet diplomats from Czechoslovakia, Romania, and Bulgaria in Israel repeatedly warned Israeli diplomats of the heavy losses that Israel would incur if war broke out. Why throw away hundreds of thousands of lives? they taunted. They generously offered the suggestion that the Soviet Union should be permitted to arbitrate between Israel and her Arab neighbors, that only Russia could guarantee peace and the security of Israel in the Middle East. Israel, they said, could rely on Russian promises, unlike those of the West.

At midnight on June 3, when the Security Council of the United Nations was called into emergency session in an attempt to forestall the onrushing war, the Soviet Ambassador, Nicholai Federenko, still confident that the three nations would stick to the script assigned them, was cavalier in his resentment at being awakened and inconvenienced for a "crisis that did not exist." Twenty-four hours later, when he realized that something had gone wrong with the scenario and the Israeli firing had begun, it was Federenko who frantically demanded an immediate emergency session of the Security Council to be called at 3 A.M. Apparently, a rude awakening.

The crucial events of April and May 1967 revealed without question the Soviet Union's prime responsibility for the Six-Day War, an example of Russian bludgeon and blunder which three years later they were ready to compound in a new round of brinkmanship over the Suez. They show how a situation can escalate beyond the control of a major power. They also show the monumental miscalculation of the Soviet leaders of the strength and determination of Israel; Russia was singularly inept in attempting to control Israel and their Arab clients at the very time she was seeking to drive a further wedge between Israelis and Arabs through which she could march into the Middle East to fill the power vacuum left by Great Britain and the United States. The unexpected collapse of the show in the Sinai drove the Kremlin to shift the play, or ploy, to an easier stage in the United States.

What the Russians lost at the Suez Canal in June 1967 they at first tried to regain on the East River of New York —and on the Potomac in Washington. How could they forget that their stunning diplomatic triumph over the combined forces of Great Britain, France, and Israel in the Suez in 1956 succeeded with the connivance of a Republican Administration in Washington (whose Vice-President is now President of the United States)?

By 1970, finding the position of the United States to be firmer than they had anticipated, the Soviet leaders decided to switch their attack from New York and Washington to the military field behind the Suez. For the first time in their history they committed Soviet pilots to air missions in a region not directly bordering on Russian soil.

SOVIET
BRINKMANSHIP

As an American diplomatic troubleshooter, I had the incredible experience through the 1960's of watching from the vantage points of the Arab capitals of Beirut, Amman, Cairo, and Damascus the Kremlin's Arab clients being maneuvered into a mere façade for the political aims of their Russian supporters. The loud, lethal weapons that I heard exploding in the Arab-Israeli combat in the Sinai were as nothing compared with the quiet Soviet political weaponry so skillfully manipulating the Arab politicians behind the battles.

For the Middle East is caught in a giant hoax. The Soviet Union's Arab client states are a mere smoke screen behind which the Kremlin's military and political aims become invisible to the world at large while it continues its push toward domination of the region.

It is not the Arabs, nor the Israelis—and decidedly not

the United States—but the Russians who are playing an increasingly dominant role in the Middle East tumult that threatens to explode into World War III. Averting one's eyes from the specter of the Russian bear crouching across the land bridge linking Europe, Asia, and Africa is nothing short of political astigmatism. For behind the *bombing* at the Suez and the *bombast* at the United Nations is the Soviet's unrelenting program to go to any lengths *short of all-out war* to prevent peace. The truth is that the Russians want neither war nor peace in the region. Either would be a severe brake on their rapid progress in gaining control of the Middle East. The real enemies of the Israelis and threat to the Middle East are not the Arab legions but the Russians who are using them as a mere façade for the multi-billion-dollar military arsenal operating under the direction of 10,000 Soviet military "advisors" behind the Suez.

From my experience in the Arab capitals, I am convinced that it is late, but still not too late, to interrupt the Soviet sweep through the Middle East. This Russian momentum can only be seen in true perspective when viewed from that country's long historic push to break out of her ice-bound isolation into warm-water ports. Having been blocked in their quest for two centuries the Soviets have since 1955 moved with ever-increasing influence in the Middle East, first at the blind and irrational invitation of Egypt's President Nasser. Now firmly rooted in the region and the power behind the Arabs, the Kremlin aims not at destroying Israel, but at capitalizing quickly on the shrinking influence of the United States in the area.

None of this is being achieved by promoting communism within the Arab states. Indeed, the Communist parties and party members in these states are expendable as far as Moscow is concerned, and no protests are heard when Communists are imprisoned in any of the Arab states of the Middle East. Communist ideology plays second fiddle to political expediency.

The Kremlin's twofold aims and actions are by now transparent: first, to build bulwarks of defense so the Middle East cannot become an opening for anti-Soviet forces on the southwest borders of the USSR; second, to build bridgeheads from which only the Russians will be able to replace those last vestiges of British influence in the area which are due to disappear with final withdrawal in 1972. In no measure does this differ from Russian aims under the czars, and is today inherent in broad Soviet policy throughout the world, including the Middle East. It is the top hinge of Soviet policy on which the door against the West turns, a door not only through which Western influence can be closed out in this area; it is a door which opens the way for creeping Soviet influence in Africa, the oil-rich Persian Gulf, and the Indian Ocean.

The Arab states, which claim Israel to be a "colony" of the West, are ready pawns in this Soviet game which has consistently fanned Arab flames of hatred and has opposed the State of Israel on all issues except the establishment of the new State in 1947. Moscow at that time saw the birth of Israel as a means of ousting the British from the region. Russia's vote alongside the voices of the Western powers two decades ago is today conveniently forgotten by the Kremlin's Arab partners in the Mideast.

Together with the massive military and economic aid Moscow is showering upon its client Arab states, Russia's consistent anti-Israel line—both within the United Nations and without—is the means by which the Soviet Union has been able to outbid the United States for the support of the Arab world. The Soviet leaders know that the United States, regardless of the extent of American economic and sympathetic ties with the Arab states, cannot in good conscience or good politics support a policy aimed at eradication of the State of Israel or any other independent state. Genocide can never become an instrument of American political policy, but it is a fair assumption that it is a tactic from which the leaders in the Kremlin would not flinch if it suited their purpose. It follows that the Soviet Union will never be outbid by the United States for Arab favor and that the Arab states will continue to look for and receive increasing Soviet support, both political and material, in their active hostility to Israel. To be forced to put her woefully tiny resources against a hundred million Arabs backed by the Soviet colossus is the crucible in which the twenty-two-year-old Israel democracy of nearly three million is being tested. Her opponent is Communist-backed Arab feudalism.

At the heart of Soviet policy, both in the Middle East and throughout the world, is fear—a fear based on the repeated invasion and brutal occupation of their land from Mongols and Teutonic knights through Napoleon to Hitler. This quality of fear is quite different from the concern of the United States, which has only once (1812–15), and then only slightly, suffered from physical invasion. Russia's nightmare of being encircled by alien forces dedicated not only to her political but even to her physical destruction is no mere fantasy. What is real and not forgotten by every Russian—not only by the party leadership and members but by all Russians—is that more than twenty-five million of them were killed by the Nazis in World War II, which is more than one in ten of the population. In defense

of their homeland against the Nazi invaders, Russian towns-
men and peasants burned their earth and crops, and destroyed their own property, causing untold misery to themselves as individuals and to the economy of their country.
Twenty-five million dead may be a blurred statistic in the
history books but not to the Russians, whose memory is
long, and for good reason. The United States has fought in
two world wars since 1918, as well as in Korea and Vietnam,
but Americans have never experienced in their own back-
yards the devastation wrought by bombs. When considering
Soviet strategy, we must never forget the national trauma
from the wounds of this experience. In the siege of Leningrad, the number of Russian dead alone was 1,250,000
persons, which is equal to the total losses the United States
has suffered in the whole of its history, including the Civil
War.

Soviet Russia's morbid fear of external enemies, which
has never abated, is in no sense a mere defensive posture.
It is obsessive. It was her insistence that eastern Europe
must never again become a foothold for anti-Soviet forces
to invade the Soviet homeland that was predominantly in
the minds of the Soviet negotiators at Yalta in 1945. Roosevelt and Churchill could not fail to have heard the finality
in the tone of Stalin's voice in 1945: "That eastern Europe
must never again become a possible foothold for German
invasion of the Soviet Union."

This, in simplest terms, also explains Soviet policy in
Czechoslovakia during the past few years. It is a fallacy to
believe that what Moscow was worried about was mere
concern at the ideological deviation of the Czech people or
government from dogmatic Marxism, Leninism, or anything
of the kind. Once a majority of the Soviet Politburo had

become convinced that the liberalization in Czechoslovakia would inevitably lead to a weakening of the bonds of the Warsaw Pact and might lead in turn to a neutralization of Czechoslovakia, constituting a threat to Russian soil, Russia was forced to act.

Ever since Stalin's rise to power, international communism has been an instrument used in the defense of the Soviet homeland. Even the slightest departure from the official Moscow party line has been regarded not in general terms as a danger to the world philosophy of Marxism, but as a specific danger to Russia herself.

It is a Soviet article of faith that there cannot be permitted to develop on its borders any possibilities of any anti-Soviet forces in Europe or in the Middle East free to invade it. Both Hungary in 1956 and Czechoslovakia in 1968 felt the blows from this anvil on which Soviet policy has been hammered out. Those two countries, both firmly within the eastern bloc, have borders contiguous to the Soviet Union. When they showed themselves as weakening links in the Soviet defense, action against them was immediate and military. The wall erected to separate East and West Germany is no mere symbolic gesture, but an actual physical division that splits the potential military power of Germany for a potential assault against Russia.

The Arab countries of the Middle East have no direct frontiers with the Soviet Union, and Soviet tactics toward them are therefore different. Seen from the Kremlin, however, the Middle East is possibly the most vulnerable area on the Soviet borderlands.

As a result of World War II, the countries of eastern Europe were established as a buffer zone in which all along the Soviet borders there was no possibility of anti-Soviet forces having any foothold directly on the Soviet borders. The line stretches from independent Finland and the three Baltic Soviet republics in the north via Poland through East Germany, Czechoslovakia, Hungary and Romania to Bulgaria on the Black Sea.

The same defense policy has been pursued consistently by the Russians in the Far East. In China, the Soviet Union took an active part in ousting pro-Western influences and was pleased to assist in the establishment of a Communist regime there. But when that Communist state showed signs of threatening the integrity of the Soviet Union, common ideology was conveniently replaced by defensive considerations.

In the two areas of the Far East where American troops have been involved since the end of World War II, both North Korea and North Vietnam are Soviet-oriented. Moving farther westward along the borders of the Soviet Union from the Far East along the subcontinent of India, the Himalaya Mountains, and the Gobi Desert—all protect the Soviet heartland from any possible alien force.

The only area in which the Soviet Union borders directly on anti-Communist or non-Communist states is the Middle East. The defensive aspect in Russia's foreign policy in the area was stressed by Soviet Foreign Minister Andrei Gromyko himself. In an address to the United Nations General Assembly on October 3, 1968, Gromyko said that the Soviet Union's interest in the Middle East was based exclusively on a security point of view; that the only area in the world from which the Soviet Union's security was directly or potentially threatened was the Middle East. Referring to Egyptian demands for Israeli withdrawal, he said: "We support this realistic proposal and are ready to assist in the implementation of such a plan to restore peace in a region directly bordering on our southern frontiers and one where the situation directly affects the security of the Soviet Union."

The Kremlin has another potent instrument to use in furthering both its defensive as well as its unacknowledged expansionist strategy in the Middle East. Although formally an atheist state, the USSR has not been unwilling to use religion and religious feelings when it suits its political and military purposes. The Russian Orthodox Church is not far removed from the Greek Orthodox Church with the important difference that the Greek Orthodox Church outside Russia is not manipulated by the Soviets. Both czarist and Soviet Russia have not hesitated to use the members of the Russian Orthodox Church as instruments for national politics and have encouraged the presence of Russian priests in Jerusalem and have shown an interest in Russian church property in the Holy Land. While there are very few Americans, or indeed any other Westerners, who are Moslems, the Soviet Union has a relatively large Moslem population of several million believers. The Russians can therefore appear to the Moslem Arabs, when they so desire, as fellow Moslems or a government interested in the fate and future of the Moslems. If and when it suits Kremlin leaders, they will have no difficulty in finding Moslem "volunteers" to fight alongside the Arabs.

The Russians have long seen the Middle East as the area of greatest potential threat to their security. When Nasser opened the door to the region, they were quick to seize the opportunity to move into the area, making reality out of an ancient Russian dream.

IV

THE PERSISTENT
THREAD—
RUSSIA'S
HISTORIC REACH
FOR POWER

The recent emergence of the Russians into the heart of the Middle East has caught the nations of the region in a sinuous web that the czars began weaving over two hundred years ago. Through the changing pattern of time, through dynasties, succeeding monarchies, revolutions, and upheavals, a persistent thread runs through Moscow's foreign policy like a warp thread in the same tapestry—the Russian drive southward toward the Black Sea and the Mediterranean.

A cynical Frenchman, surveying the results of a revolution in his own country, summed it up with the truism: "The more it changes, the more it remains the same."

A close-up of over two hundred years of the Russians' southward pattern reveals a series of failures that would have long since unstrung a lesser people's policy. But Russian tenacity, seeing failures as merely temporary detours, continues to press toward its southern destinations from the czars of all the Russians—past the Bolshevik Revolution, through the Stalin and Khrushchev regimes as it continues to stir up the warm waters of the Middle East into a violent hurricane.

The Russian Bolshevik Revolution of 1917, a cataclysmic upheaval, might well have twisted this thread and reversed the directions of Russian foreign policy. And indeed, for the first few years when the World Revolution philosophy of Lenin and Trotsky dominated Soviet aims, the web was spread wide into a world network. But during the Stalin and post-Stalin eras the old thread was again tightened to restore the pattern of the national Russian policy-mosaic— the drive southward to warm-water ports with Turkey as the conduit.

I was able to watch at close hand from a sensitive diplomatic post at the U.S. embassy in Ankara in 1944 and 1945 while Turkey played the climax of the Second World War by ear, as it were, calling itself "neutral" until the last months of the war. From a ringside seat in Ankara, I observed the dizzy crosscurrents of political espionage as it was played by the greedy Turkish politicians in collaboration with the evil genius Franz von Papen, Hitler's agent. Throughout most of World War II the Turks sat on the sidelines profiting from both sides, but anticipating a German victory. In the summer of 1944, when the tide turned swiftly in favor of the Allies, it was a lesson in political acrobatics to watch the Turks do a virtual policy somersault. Overnight they abandoned their fake neutrality and rushed to the side of the Allies. Thus the Turks were able to maintain their possessions intact, including Istanbul (Constantinople). They also managed to sneak in as a founder-member of the United Nations. Again, just as they were within reach of their coveted prize-city, the Russians were foiled.

For over three centuries the Ottoman Empire had held dominion over the area that stretches from the Balkans to Egypt. The beginnings of Ottoman decline in the nineteenth century offered the British, French, and Russians an opportunity to divide the spoils and brought the three powers into constant clash with one another.

Constantinople (now Istanbul) and what was Palestine were the springboards from which the great powers sought to expand their empires, and for good reason. For this region is the nerve center of communications between three continents, a land bridge between Asia, Africa, and Europe. Even today, when the Suez Canal has lost its importance as a channel between Europe, East Africa, and the Far East, airplanes must land at Tel Aviv, Beirut, Cairo, or Istanbul en route to Africa and Asia. The Russian czars had long whetted their appetites to gobble up this overripe falling plum. Istanbul at the fountainhead of Turkey was the pivotal opening for Russian entry into the Middle East. Constantinople and the Dardanelles had to be denied to the Russians. As the Ottoman Empire disintegrated, it is not difficult to see why the major world powers moved in to establish bases there. But again and again, as the Russians were poised to pounce on Istanbul, history even to this very day has managed to withhold the jewel on the Golden Horn from the Kremlin's grasp.

Nor was the prize remote from the ambitions of Frederick the Great, Bismarck, and Wilhelm II, who, at the turn of the twentieth century, saw the crossroads to the East as protection of Germany's African colonies and the key to expansion of its power into the region. No mere shibboleth or empty slogan was *Drang nach Osten* with its planned rail link to the famed Orient Express—a two-day journey from Paris to the Balkans and Constantinople—and beyond to Baghdad. This great luxury train, the scene of many thrilling spy mysteries, was at that time the only means of travel from Europe into the Balkans, terminating at Istanbul, where espionage thrived at the threshold of Asia Minor.

The "Eastern Question," which has long occupied historians, is the general term used to describe the political relations of the West with the Ottoman Empire for more than four centuries. The beginnings of this "question," as far as Russia is concerned, are to be traced back to Peter the Great (1682–1725), who transformed Russia from a relatively unimportant quasi-Asiatic country into a major European power. He did this by formulating a policy of expansion westward against Sweden (of which the construction of St. Petersburg, his "window to the West," was part) and southward toward the warm-water ports of the Black Sea. Peter's interest in Europe had been aroused by his study tour of the courts of Europe; his strategic interests in Constantinople were in part based on the affinity between the Russian Orthodox and the Greek Orthodox churches. It was not, however, until the reign of Catherine II (1762–1796) that Russia's interest in the already decaying Ottoman Empire came into sharp focus, in the first two of the Russo-Turkish wars (1768–74 and 1787–92), fought with the aim of capturing Constantinople. To help her expansionist ambitions in the Middle East, Catherine used the Mohammedan faith to win her friends in this Islamic area. In 1785 she published a charter of toleration of Islam and encouraged Moslem and medieval Mohammedan learning among the Kirghiz and other tribes which had come under Russian domination.

A sudden tactical switch in the middle of the series of wars between Russia and Turkey brought the two countries into temporary alliance in 1833, when Russia aided Turkey (an ironic twist of the thread) against Mohammed Ali of Egypt. The joining of these two powers was seen by Great Britain as a dangerous threat to her imperial routes to the Far East. For one of the major tenets of British policy for over two centuries—the maintenance of her overseas communications with India—brought her into repeated conflict with Russia's Middle Eastern ambitions. This clash came to a climax in the Crimean War of 1854–56, which blossomed from a dispute between Russia and France over the Holy Places in Palestine.

In 1850 a quarrel broke out in Bethlehem, which was under Ottoman rule, between Russia and France, in the interests of the Greek Orthodox Church and the Roman Catholic Church respectively, concerning the right to mark with a star the birthplace of Christ in the church of the Nativity. Russia aimed to color the star at Bethlehem in its own hue. Czar Nicholas I, who saw in this an opportunity to extend Russian influence in the Mediterranean, demanded from Sultan Abdul Medjid of Turkey not merely the guardianship of the Holy Places, but also a protectorate over all Orthodox Catholics in the sultan's dominions—a concession that would have reduced Turkey to Russian vassalage. The sultan considered Russia's occupation of the Danubian principalities an act of war, and therefore declared war against Russia (1853). The sultan appealed to France and

Great Britain for aid: their favorable response involved all four powers in the Crimean War (1854–56).

France challenged Russia's claims to guardianship over these sites in the Holy Land. While Britain's ostensible aim in going to war against Russia was to protect the Turks in the Danubian provinces from the invading Russians, the British press at the time frankly admitted that the real aim was to destroy Sebastopol to end Russian naval power in the Black Sea, so that Britain's lifeline would not be threatened.

Twenty years later, during another period of Russo-British friction when their policies again collided in the Mediterranean, British aims were revealed in a London music-hall song which gave the world the expression "Jingo" (for a rabid patriot). The ditty which went "We don't want to fight but, by Jingo if we do, we've got the ships, we've got the men, we've got the money too" ends with the refrain: "The Russians shall not have Constantinople." Some years later, and a century ago, Russia's reply was given by Dostoievsky in his *Diary of a Writer*: "Constantinople must be ours, even if it should take another century."

Dostoievsky's prophetic century has now passed, and modern Russia—the Soviet Union—is still striving for the Middle Eastern prize.

It was Czar Nicholas I who coined the phrase "The Sick Man of Europe" to describe the Turkish sultanate, and in World War I Czar Nicholas was still planning to pick up the pieces of the sinking Ottoman Empire. He obtained from the Allies the promise that Constantinople be given to Russia at the successful conclusion of the war as his part of the spoils.

But the Bolshevik Revolution of 1917 prevented the Russians from pressing their claim. Even after the czar was deposed in February 1917, the new Provisional Government affirmed the original secret pact with the Allies under which Russia was to have control of Constantinople and the Turkish Straits. Revelation of this helped overthrow Paul Milyukov, the Liberal foreign minister, and was a prime factor in the overthrow of the Kerensky government by Lenin.

Isolated from Europe in the early days of the revolutionary government, the Soviet Union began again looking toward the Mediterranean warm-water ports. Step by step, she pressed southward. By 1920 Iran had been "liberated" from British influence; a treaty was signed by the Kremlin in 1921, outlining how the Soviet Union could send troops to Iran to forestall an attack by other powers. The following year, Moscow helped destroy British influence in Egypt; in 1925 the Soviet Union signed a treaty of neutrality and nonaggression with Turkey; and in 1928 she signed neutrality treaties with Iran, and with Yemen, one of the most backward countries in the whole world, but a back door to the Persian Gulf and oil-rich Saudi Arabia, a door which to this day she is attempting to pry open.

In 1931 and 1932, the Kremlin signed commercial and naval treaties with Turkey and in 1936 was a cosignatory of the Montreux Convention, which granted the USSR and other signatory nations shipping rights through the Dardanelles and the Bosporus, the straits linking the Black Sea with the Mediterranean. To some extent the special terms given the Soviet Union were similar to those promised the czar during World War I: Russia was permitted to send her warships through the straits in peacetime, but had to give eight days' notice of such passage. This has always griped the Russians, who interpret it as a block against their ambition to the south. Foiled in attempts to amend the treaty in her favor, Moscow has since managed to circumvent these restrictions by placing permanent notification on record in Turkey that Red Fleet vessels will pass through the straits. These standby lists sent to the Turkish government at regular intervals have now become routine and have given the Soviet Union the means of bolstering her Mediterranean fleet without interference.

Stalin entertained no scruples at the outset of World War II in following the "imperialist intrigues" of Czar Nicholas II when it came to picking up the thread of Russia's drive to the warm-water ports of the Black Sea and the Mediterranean. The Ribbentrop-Molotov pact, negotiated and signed in November 1940, agreed "that the area south of Batum and Baku in the general direction of the Persian Gulf is recognized as the center of the aspirations of the Soviet Union." The full story of this period, when Nazi Germany and the Soviet Union were allies, has not yet been told. But enough has been revealed by the Department of State publication of the protocols of the pact to show that the Russians made no secret to their Nazi allies that Soviet ambitions in the Middle East coincided exactly with Czarist ambitions and with Russia's historic push southward.

V

THE WEST
SLOWS
SOVIET
AMBITIONS

It was not until World War II that the United States was finally brought into major involvement in the Middle East and began to appreciate the growing strategic importance of the area. Without the Middle East as a major center of communications and of petroleum resources, Great Britain could not have brought World War II to a successful conclusion. When, after the fall of Tobruk in June 1942, President Roosevelt asked Churchill what he could do to help, his blunt reply was: "Give us as many Sherman tanks as you can spare and ship them to the Middle East as quickly as possible." Roosevelt's swift dispatch of these new tanks to Field Marshal Montgomery and the black-bereted leader's massed artillery helped stop Field Marshal Rommel at El Alamein and turned the tide of the war.

In the Grand War Alliance of the United States, Great Britain, and the Soviet Union, it was necessary to get aid and supplies to the Soviet Union by occupying neutral Iran. War materiel was also pumped by the United States into the Soviet Union through Murmansk in the north. But that Arctic port was icebound for many months of the year. The only twelve-month corridor was through the southern warm-water ports of Basra in Iraq and Abadan and Bandar Shah-pur in Iran.

Control of the Iranian supply line was given to the U.S. Army Engineers, who performed magnificent feats of logistics. Teheran was the scene of some of the only friendly meetings between the officers and the men of the United States and the Soviet Union. American transport of the war matériel to the Red Army enabled it to withstand the Nazi assault. Although the Soviet Union was rescued by these supplies, it took advantage of its position to recall its 1925 treaty of neutrality in an attempt to occupy Iran's northern provinces. After the war the Soviets also demanded oil concessions in northern Iran, and in 1944 Russia even challenged the presence in Iran of the very American troops who were bringing her lend-lease supplies.

At the Potsdam Conference after the end of the war in Europe, Stalin gave his personal assurance to President Truman that he had no designs on Iran. But instead, he renewed his demand for a revision of the Montreux Convention and pressed his claims further, demanding joint control of the Dardanelles Strait and bases in Turkey.

These aggressive Soviet moves in Iran and Turkey, along with Kremlin encouragement of the Communist rebellion in Greece, convinced President Truman that a Russian offensive toward the Middle East was in the making, the final goal being control of Iran. Together with the threat of a Communist coup in Greece, it looked like a giant pincers movement against the oil-rich areas of the Middle East and the warm-water ports of the Mediterranean.

On February 21, 1947, Great Britain informed the United States that she could no longer bear the financial burden of aiding the Greek and Turkish governments and would pull out by March 30. At the same time, British negotiations with the Arabs and Jews in the Holy Land were deadlocked, and Great Britain referred the Palestine question to the United Nations. Clearly, Great Britain's historic control of the Middle East was slipping away.

By 1947, the United States began to assume the mantle dropped by England as the dominant force in the Middle East. A subtle shift away from Great Britain had really begun during the war, as Roosevelt gradually became more and more independent of Churchill's political ideas. At the same time, America's economic interests in the area deepened with the establishment of ARAMCO (Arabian-American Oil Company) and TAPline (Trans-Arabian Pipeline), the oil-prospecting, -producing, and -transportation corporations with their important and influential lobbies on Capitol Hill.

President Truman saw in the ambitious moves of the Russians a new, dangerous menace to peace. In eastern Europe, the agreements made at Yalta and Potsdam were ignored. In the Middle East, Russia made territorial demands on Turkey, aided the armed rebellion of Greek Communists, and kept her troops in Iran to encourage a Kurdistan revolt against the Iranian monarchy. This was contrary to Stalin's agreement with Roosevelt to pull her troops out of Iran immediately after the end of the war. Only strong pressure from the United States finally forced Stalin to withdraw Russian troops from Iran.

The United States at first met this aggression by supporting Turkey in her resistance to Soviet demands and by backing Iran in her determination to evict the Russians from her territory. The Soviet occupation of Iran had come about during an attempted pro-Nazi revolt in neighboring Iraq (the Rashid Ali putsch) while Stalin and Hitler were allies. Captured German Foreign Office documents had revealed to United States policy makers the continued territorial ambitions of the Russians in the Middle East. The United States now realized that Stalin was trying to make the same gains he had sought in the Mideast when he had been Hitler's ally. For the Russians, the secret Middle East clauses of the Molotov-Ribbentrop Pact remain valid to this very day.

The Truman Doctrine was conceived to meet the immediate Soviet threat to Greece and Turkey. Billions were poured into those two countries from United States coffers and succeeded in pushing the Soviets back from their destined warm-water ports. But the Truman Doctrine didn't stop there. It called for the general containment of Soviet Communist expansion anywhere in the world. This worldwide call to arms was considered necessary to arouse both the Congress and the American people from the euphoria of good will toward their late Soviet ally and to dispel the naïve American feeling that the end of the war would also end world power politics. The United States could no longer continue its traditional postwar policy of disarmament.

On May 22, 1947, Congress overwhelmingly approved four hundred million dollars in aid to Greece and Turkey for the first year. Even more significant was the establishment of the Sixth Fleet in the Mediterranean as watchdog and shield for the United States, which had by now become inextricably involved in the Middle East. President Truman's foresight was rewarded when, in 1958, President Eisenhower ordered the Sixth Fleet to unload regiments of American marines on the shores of Lebanon barely in time to snatch this tiny Western-controlled nation from the jaws of Nasser's voracious pan-Arab appetite. Today, the Sixth Fleet still dominates the Mediterranean seas but is increasingly shadowed by the expanding Russian Navy, whose principal bases are now Alexandria and Port Said in Egypt, Latakia in Syria, and Algiers. The American ships are also kept under close surveillance by Russian jet aircraft based on Egyptian airfields. Some, while flown by Soviet pilots, are camouflaged with Egyptian markings. Now, Soviet pilots not only keep watch over the Sixth Fleet, but have also taken over the complete aerial defense of Cairo, Alexandria, and the Aswân Dam. Russia's toehold on the shores of the Middle East has now become a foothold.

RUSSIA
ARRIVES
IN THE
MIDDLE
EAST

VI

RUSSIA
VOTES FOR
ISRAEL'S BIRTH
TO OUST
GREAT BRITAIN

It was the Russians' "Da" together with the "Yes" votes of the United States and the Western World against the opposition of the Arab members of the United Nations that called Israel into being. Today the Russo-Arab bloc would now like nothing better than to overlook Moscow's historic partition vote in the General Assembly on November 29, 1947.

The free world voted to establish Israel in part of the former territory of Palestine mandated to England because they felt that it offered a fair way of dealing with the conflict in the area between the Arabs and the Jews.

Russia's vote, however, was not concerned with helping the Jewish people. Moscow saw in the dilemma put before the United Nations a chance to bring Russia nearer to control of the warm-water ports of the Mediterranean and the Middle East by ousting one of the last vestiges of British power in the land-bridge area linking Europe, Africa, and Asia.

The peoples of the Middle East are ancient—among the most ancient in the world—but the countries and present political entities in that area are among some of the newest states of the United Nations. The Holy Land was the most popular subject for the prolific cartographers of the fifteenth and sixteenth centuries. Today their colorful products adorn the walls of many houses. On them, and around the borders of the area described variously as "Holy Land," "Palestine," or "Land of Israel," may sometimes be found reference to Egypt and Babylon (the forerunner of modern Iraq). But search as you may, nothing can be found relating to the political entities of Lebanon, Syria, and Jordan among Israel's modern neighbors or of Saudi Arabia or Yemen further afield. For these are all countries called into being during the past four or five decades, to suit the political and imperial needs of Britain and France. Few natural lines delineate their borders, which were drawn up in secret negotiations between the powers. In certain cases, they were carved out merely to provide a throne for a dependent tribal leader, for services rendered to one or other of the imperial powers vying for strategic bases in the area, or to fulfill wartime promises to purchase aid in the World War I struggle against the Turks.

From the early days of the sixteenth century the Middle East had been under the domination of the Ottoman Empire until the defeat of Turkey by the Allies in World War I. The spoils fell to Britain and France mainly in the form of mandates granted by the League of Nations.

Ottoman rule over Egypt had lasted from 1517 until the

British occupation in World War I with a brief interregnum under Napoleon Bonaparte from 1798 to 1801 and British occupation in 1882, when a British "resident governor" was installed, although the country nominally continued under Turkish rule. Great Britain maintained its control over Egypt, which it had wrested from the Turks in the nineteenth century, even while the country was still nominally governed from Constantinople.

Under the Versailles Treaty, France was granted control of the Levant States of Syria and Lebanon, while Great Britain was granted the mandate for Palestine, a large area stretching from the Mediterranean to the borders of the newly carved-out kingdom of Iraq. In 1921 the British unilaterally decided to partition part of its mandated area. "Over a cup of tea," as Winston Churchill was later to describe it, London decided to carve off the area east of the Jordan River to provide a throne in Amman for its protégé, the Emir Abdullah. The Emirate of Transjordan (abbreviated to Jordan), the region west of the Jordan River, became, under the UN partition plan, an independent Arab state parallel to Israel. It was incorporated by the Amman monarch and was officially declared "Independent under the Mandate" in 1923.

France's zone of influence was laid down in an Anglo-French secret treaty negotiated in 1916, and the mandated area entrusted to Paris covered both modern Syria and Lebanon—the "Levant States." A political border between the two states was drawn in 1920 to give separate autonomy to the predominantly Christian area of Lebanon, away from Moslem Syria. In 1926 Syria declared itself a republic with French assent but under French control, while in 1930 Lebanon also became an independent republic under the

French mandate. Both Syria and Lebanon obtained their independence in World War II.

Egypt was declared a British protectorate in 1914 (to protect the British interests in the Suez Canal) and was granted independence in 1922, though still under British military control. Under the terms of the Constantinople Convention of 1888, the Suez Canal was scheduled to be handed over to complete Egyptian control in 1968.

It was Palestine which remained the longest under foreign imperial rule. The region lying west of the Jordan River in which Britain, during World I, had promised to facilitate the establishment of a National Home for the Jewish People has sometimes been described cynically as the "twice-promised land." The Arabs claimed that British promises made to them also covered this same area. From 1921 onward the area was rent by strife and bloodshed, with Arab attacks on Jewish areas and the British maintaining a pro-Arab neutrality, whittling away the promises inscribed in the Balfour Declaration. During this period several attempts were made to find a way between the apparently contradictory promises. All solutions were based on one form or another of partition into Jewish and Arab states. In 1937, the British Royal Commission, headed by Lord Peel, made a recommendation that was accepted by the Jews of Palestine but with misgivings, as it was less than they had hoped for. But it was rejected by the Arab leadership. The recommendation findings had first been accepted by the British Government.

With the outbreak of World War II the Jewish leaders of Palestine called a truce with the British Government in order to participate in the war against the common enemy—Nazi Germany. Over 30,000 men and women out of the country's 600,000 Jews volunteered for service in Palestine Jewish units of the British army and fought with their Western allies in North Africa and Europe. Only a handful of Arabs, however, could be found to volunteer, though the Grand Mufti of Jerusalem, Haj Amin el-Husseini, even paid a ceremonial call on Hitler in Berlin to offer the services of the Arabs in the Nazi cause.

In 1943 Britain dumped the "Palestine problem" into the lap of the United Nations, successor organization to the League of Nations, which had granted the original mandate. Young and vigorous as it was in those early days, the United Nations acted with great speed. A special General Assembly was summoned in April 1947 and within two weeks, on May 15, 1947, established NUSCOP—the UN Special Committee on Palestine—with instructions to investigate the problem and propose a solution by September 1, in time for the regular General Assembly session that winter. With the energy and health of the world organization in those halcyon days the report was ready on time, after the committee had carried out an on-the-spot investigation in the Middle East and elsewhere. The solution it found was similar to that of the Peel Commission ten years earlier—to partition Palestine into two states, one Jewish and another Arab, with a special international regime for Jerusalem. All were to be linked in economic union.

For two months a hard, realistic debate raged within the United Nations. When the vote was taken on November 29, 1947, 33 members voted in favor, 13 against, with ten abstentions. The negative votes were cast by the then six Arab UN members and four other Moslem states, as well as by Cuba, Greece, and India. The Soviet Union lined up alongside the United States in favor; Britain abstained.

Moscow not only voted for the partition resolution; it worked hard and vociferously to ensure its passage. Reversing for a moment a long history of hostility toward the Jewish people and any rights to its own homeland, Andrei Gromyko stole the headlines with a ringing speech at the United Nations supporting the creation of a Jewish state in Palestine:

> The fact that no Western European nation found the strength to guarantee the rights of the Jewish people to defend [themselves] from the clutches of the fascist hangmen explains the passion of the Jews to have a homeland of their own . . . not to recognize this would be an injustice and to deny this passion its fulfillment would be wholly indefensible.

Six weeks before the partition vote was taken the Soviet representative to the Special ad hoc Committee of the United Nations Assembly discussing the question, Tsarapkin, said:

> The Jewish people are, therefore, striving to create a state of their own, and it would be unjust to deny them that right. . . . Every people—and that includes the Jewish people—has the full right to demand that their fate should not depend on the mercy or the goodwill of a particular state.

Gromyko returned to the verbal fray on November 26, three days before the vote:

> The delegation of the USSR maintains that the decision to partition Palestine is in keeping with the high principles and aims of the United Nations. It is in keeping with the principle of the national self-determination of peoples. . . . The solution of the Palestine problem based on a partition of Palestine into two separate States will be of profound historical significance

because this decision will meet the legitimate demands of the
Jewish people. [UN Document A/PV 125]

The Soviet delegate had no sympathy for the Arabs who
were trying desperately to block the establishment of Israel
(and who were shortly to follow up their verbal assault by
open warfare). Gromyko said:

> The representatives of the Arab states claim that the partition
> of Palestine would be an historic injustice. But this view of the
> case is unacceptable, if only because, after all, the Jewish
> people has been closely linked with Palestine for a considerable
> period in history. [UN Document A/PV 125]

Fully aware of the Soviet aim, which was solely to hasten
the departure of Western influence from the eastern Mediterranean, the Western powers found themselves faced with
the alternatives of supporting the Russian line or of opposing
establishment of the Jewish State. To get out of the dilemma,
the Americans proposed a temporary trusteeship in place of
the plan to partition Palestine, which had been approved by
the General Assembly. The United States delegate, Warren
Austin, called for a new General Assembly meeting to establish a "United Nations trusteeship" over Palestine on the
grounds that the situation in Palestine was rapidly becoming
perilous and that a peaceful partition of the area between
Arabs and Jews appeared remote, if not impossible. This
trusteeship as a substitute for partition became the main
thrust of American policy throughout the months preceding
Israel's establishment.

But the Soviet delegation vigorously opposed the trusteeship. Moscow saw it as a continuation of Western influence.
Russian spokesmen challenged the American claim that there

was no possibility of a peaceful solution, hammering away at the contention that the American position would leave both the Arabs and Jews of Palestine without a state of their own and would serve the economic and strategic interests of the big powers rather than the United Nations.

The debate within the United Nations raged while the Palestine Commission reported to the Security Council on February 16, 1948:

> Powerful Arab interests, both inside and outside of Palestine, are defying the resolution of the General Assembly and are engaged in a deliberate effort to alter by force the settlement envisaged therein. [Doc. s/676]

On April 16, 1948, the special meeting of the General Assembly convened to discuss the American trusteeship proposal and referred it to the Trusteeship Council five days later. The United Nations bodies debated and procrastinated. But the tide of events was moving inexorably toward partitioning Palestine in two—an Arab and a Jewish state. Only one month remained before the British would complete their withdrawal from Palestine on May 15. By the time the Assembly began its debate on the American proposal of a limited trusteeship over the Jerusalem area, only one hour remained before the end of the British mandate and the formal proclamation of the establishment of the State of Israel. A few precious minutes passed in procedural discussions. The USSR objected to the Assembly President's limit of five minutes per speaker. More time passed as representatives of the Ukraine, Egypt, Iraq, Poland, Afghanistan, and Yemen spoke out against the Jerusalem trusteeship. France and the United States supported the proposal. As the voting began, the Syrian delegation noted that it was one minute after six (midnight in Palestine), and "The whole game was up." The American proposal failed to gain the necessary two-thirds vote and was defeated, leaving the original partition proposal of separate Arab and Jewish states as the only General Assembly resolution for Palestine.

The Soviet Union had succeeded in defeating the American trusteeship device, not by its ability to muster votes, but by sidetracking discussions, prolonging debate, and delaying decisions. This was a strategy Moscow would use again and again on Middle East issues in the United Nations to suit its purposes. Meanwhile, back in the Middle East, a few hours after the end of the British mandate and the declaration of the establishment of the State of Israel, the then secretary general of the Arab League, Azzam Pasha, told a press conference in Cairo that the aim of the Arabs was the "extermination and momentous massacre" of the Jews. At the same time the Egyptian foreign minister cabled the Security Council:

> The Royal Egyptian Government declares, now that the British Mandate in Palestine has ended, that the Egyptian armed forces have started to enter Palestine. [UN Doc. S/743]

The bellicose statements and belligerent actions of the Arabs were sharply attacked by Soviet spokesmen in the United Nations. Gromyko told the Security Council on May 18, 1948:

> Everyone knows that military operations are now taking place in Palestine, that there is fighting between the Arabs and the Jews, that the regular troops of several Arab states have entered Palestine territory and are carrying out military operations there. [UN Doc. 2/PV 295]

Three days later he repeated:

The USSR delegation cannot but express surprise at the position adopted by the Arab States in the Palestine question, and particularly at the fact that those States—or some of them, at least—have resorted to such action as sending out their troops into Palestine and carrying out military operations aimed at the suppression of the national liberation movement in Palestine." [Official Records—Security Council, 3rd year No. 71, 299th meeting, Page 7]

Moscow was ably supported by its Soviet satellites. Tarassenco, the Ukrainian UN delegate, told the Security Council on May 20, 1948:

We are concerned with the plain fact that a number of Palestine's neighbor states have sent their troops into Palestine. Our knowledge of that fact is not based on rumors, or on newspaper reports, but on official documents signed by the Governments of those States informing the Security Council that their troops have entered Palestine. I refer, in particular, to the documents signed and sent by the Governments of Egypt and Transjordan. [UN Doc. S/PV 295]

A week later he asked:

What can the Security Council do today? It can only note the same situation as it did on May 17, namely that an armed struggle is taking place in Palestine as a result of the unlawful invasion by a number of States of the territory of Palestine, which does not form part of the territory of any of the States whose armed forces have invaded it. [UN Doc. S/PV 306]

The following day Tarassenco again said:

I would point out, in the first place, that we do not know of a single case of the invasion of the territory of another State by the armed forces of Israel, except in self-defense, where they had to beat off attacks by the armed forces of other States on Israel territory. That was self-defense in the full sense of the word. [UN Doc. S/PV 307]

Gromyko did not let his allies carry the ball alone. On July 7 he himself told the Security Council:

World public opinion has already condemned the action of certain Arab circles who attacked the Jewish State and occupied the territory allotted to the Arab State in Palestine. [UN Doc. S/PV 331]

In those early days the Soviet representatives minced no words in their condemnation of the Arab actions which they apparently feared might reverse Moscow's plans to oust the British. Gromyko told the Security Council on May 29, 1948:

This is not the first time that the Arab States, which organized the invasion of Palestine, have ignored a decision of the Security Council or of the General Assembly. The USSR delegation deems it essential that the Council should state its opinion more clearly and more firmly with regard to this attitude of the Arab States towards decisions of the Security Council. It is not in the interest of the United Nations in general, or of the Security Council in particular, to tolerate such a situation, where decisions of the Council designed to put an end to warfare—and the Palestine events can only be described as warfare—are being flouted. These decisions are being completely ignored by the Governments primarily responsible for the present situation in Palestine." [UN Doc. S/PV 309]

A year after the partition vote the Byelorussian delegate Kiseleve told the United Nations General Assembly on November 24, 1948: "Like other States before it, Israel was born of an armed struggle for liberty and independence."

Moscow's vigorous support of Israel and its hostility to the Arabs was to be of short duration. The Soviet's "Da" in the General Assembly had, indeed, led to the departure of the British from Palestine. But the Israelis had not provided the Russians with the "partnership" or invitation they sought for entry into the Mediterranean area. The Arabs have a saying: "The enemy of my enemy is my friend." What the Israelis refused to give Moscow, Colonel Nasser would.

VII

SOVIET
SOMERSAULT

The Soviet-Israeli honeymoon was brief. Despite a long history of anti-Zionism and active anti-Semitism within the USSR, the Soviet leaders felt that the liberal orientation of Israel and the social philosophy of the Kibbutz movement would ensure Israel's support of the Soviet Union.

Israel's leadership was not taken in by this Kremlin ploy. Moscow had apparently counted on Israeli gratitude. Even during this period, anti-Semitism was prevalent in Russia. At the very moment that Russian spokesmen in the United Nations were defending the establishment of Israel, denouncing Arab aggression, and supporting Israel's application for membership in the United Nations, the Jews of the Soviet Union were undergoing what the Soviet-Jewish writer Ilya Ehrenburg later recalled as "the most difficult days of my entire life." Stalin's purge resulted in the arrest and murder of leading Jewish writers, the disbanding of the

Jewish Anti-Fascist Committee in the Soviet Union, and the closing down of its newspaper.

Nor was this Soviet anti-Jewish campaign limited to Russia. It included all the countries under Soviet control and became part of a general denunciation of the "international Zionist-Capitalist conspiracy." Its peak came with the infamous "doctors' plot." Acting upon Stalin's orders, the Soviet secret police arrested and tortured a number of leading Soviet medical men, most of them Jews, charging them with an attempt to assassinate prominent Soviet officials. After Stalin's death, the Soviet authorities branded these charges as fraudulent, and a number of Soviet police officials were executed for complicity in the frame-up.

The first sign of the Kremlin's disenchantment with Israel came within months of the establishment of Israel. The Jewish State's first minister to Moscow was Golda Meyerson (later, Golda Meir, the present prime minister of Israel). Upon her arrival at Moscow airport she was mobbed by scores of thousands of Russian Jews who turned out to greet her. Her appearance in the Moscow synagogue on the first Sabbath after her arrival in the Russian capital became a spontaneous demonstration of love and affection for the new Hebrew-speaking state on the part of many thousands of Jews, both old and young. Jews who had been oppressed by both czar and commissar kissed the hand of this representative of the independent Jewish State. Stalin, who had started his political career in the Soviet State as a commissar for national minorities and who had claimed to have solved the "minorities problem," suddenly discovered that the only minority problem he had not solved was that of the Jews. Indeed, Russia's support for partition and the establishment of Israel had led to a strengthening of the conviction of the

Jews of the Soviet Union for their own national identity.

Within the United Nations itself, the Soviet Union, despairing of capturing Israel as a satellite or of even detaching her from sympathy to the West, embarked on a wait-and-see attitude while fishing for new opportunities.

The change in Soviet tactics began in 1949 when Russia joined the Arab bloc in the United Nations and reaffirmed a resolution calling for the internationalization of Jerusalem. This came over the protests of Jordan, which had seized the Old City of Jerusalem during the 1948 fighting and refused to give it up to any outside control. The Arab States reciprocated the favor in 1950 when Egypt, as a member of the Security Council, abstained in a Western-sponsored vote to condemn Communist aggression in Korea. In another Western-sponsored vote in the General Assembly to name Communist China as an aggressor following participation of Chinese volunteers in the Korean War, Egypt, Saudi Arabia, Syria, and Yemen abstained.

By 1952, the Soviets had swung to the Arab side. A United Nations resolution calling for the Israeli and Arab governments to enter into direct negotiations to resolve their differences passed the special *ad hoc* Political Committee of the General Assembly with the Soviet bloc abstaining. When the resolution came to the General Assembly and appeared to have a good chance of passing, the Soviets switched from abstention to opposition, killing any chance of gaining the necessary two-thirds approval. The Soviets demonstrated their ability to play the role of spoiler, preventing the passage of any resolution that they disapproved of, while lacking the strength to pass resolutions of their own.

In 1954, at the height of the Prague trials of Jews charged with "Zionist and imperialist activities against the Communist State," a bomb was thrown into the Soviet legation in Tel Aviv. Moscow promptly broke off its diplomatic relations with Israel. For the Arabs, this was convincing proof that Moscow had changed its 1947–48 attitudes and could be wooed.

The Soviet Union found the partner it was looking for in the Middle East in the person of the new leader of Egypt, Abdel Gamal Nasser. By his own description "a hero in search of a role" Nasser proved to be politically adaptable in playing the United States against the Soviet to advance his ambition to lead the Arab world. The Soviets, no less obliging, were willing to overlook any of Nasser's ideological leanings as long as he was anti-Western.

This was the door that opened the present Soviet alliance with the Arab countries, which in the United Nations has since resulted in almost automatic Soviet support for Arab interests. In the Middle East itself the Russian fleet has sailed into the Mediterranean, Soviet pilots have gone to Egypt, and the Kremlin has come within sight of ousting United States oil interests from the region. In January 1954 the Russians gave Syrian dictator Abed Shishakly's government full support in the Security Council to block Israel's plan to drain the Hula swamps and use the Jordan River waters for irrigation. (Later Shishakly was condemned by Moscow as an agent of Western imperialism.) Shortly after, the Soviets also vetoed a New Zealand resolution calling for freedom of passage in the Suez Canal and blocked the transfer of this question to the Israel-Egypt mixed armistice commission, where Israel and Egypt might have solved the problem face to face. The Jordanian parliament, surprised and delighted by their newfound champion, responded by voting Andrei Vishinsky, the Soviet foreign minister, an unprecedented resolution of thanks for support of the Arab cause in the Security Council.

As social ferment and anti-Western sentiment increased in the Arab countries, the Soviets pressed their advantage.

In 1954 and 1955 acrobatics at the United Nations began and led to the Kremlin's eventual complete political somersault from its 1947–48 position. This was the time of the emergence of the "third world" as a potential force in politics, the period of the Bandung Conference in which a growing number of Asian and African states were entering the United Nations and influencing its decisions. Under Nikita Khrushchev's leadership the Russians were taking their first steps in the foreign-aid game. At the United Nations, the Kremlin, which had originally boycotted the Trusteeship Council and had entered it only reluctantly to pursue their aims in Palestine, now emerged as the self-appointed champion of all the newly independent territories. While the more sophisticated observer may have seen through the transparent Soviet posturings, the efforts to influence the emerging nations succeeded.

Many of the underdeveloped nations turned to the Soviet Union as their model for social organization, industrial development at a rapid rate, and mobilization of their population to support their policies. The rise of leftist or socialist governments in many African and Asian states convinced the Soviets that it was only a matter of time until this "third world" was absorbed into the Communist camp. And as this conviction grew, appeals to the Soviet for support from the new nations grew. In 1956 the Russians had suggested independence for all trust territories in three to five years. In 1960, a Soviet-drafted "Declaration on the granting of Independence to all colonial countries" proclaimed that the trusteeship system must be "buried together with the entire obsolete system of colonialism," and demanded an immediate end to all dependencies. To Egyptians, Syrians, and Iraqi this was attractive oratory.

During the summer of 1956, only weeks before the Suez war, Dmitri Shepilov, then Soviet foreign minister, blocked any debate on Israel's right to transit through the Suez Canal by claiming that "Egypt does not want to close the canal— therefore freedom of passage is not an issue." The Soviets then vetoed a Security Council resolution proposing a Canal-Users' Association, leaving matters at an impasse which eventually led to war. Where United Nations discussions or findings fitted Soviet needs, the Russians could be super-supporters of international arbitration. But as in October of 1955, United Nations observers found Egypt responsible for tensions along the border with Israel. "This," as the Soviet journal *International Life* put it, "is not to be taken seriously, for the Egyptian Army has denied the charges."

Only later, in 1967, with the advent of the Six-Day War would the Russians come full circle, rewrite history, and condemn Israel as the sole aggressor in 1948.

Since then, the Kremlin has lost no opportunity to malign and threaten Israel as the aggressor, castigating her at the United Nations, in her strident press and in her replies to United States notes. The Soviet main tactic has been to put pressure on the United States to impose terms on Israel to withdraw from the Arab occupied zones via a so-called Big Four, including France and England. By accepting this Big Power formula, the United States has unfortunately played into the hands of the Russians, accepting them as equal Mideast partners in meeting to formulate so-called peace terms. This political tactic has only resulted in endless futile meetings with the United States, but it has encouraged the Arabs to look for a settlement in their favor from the Big Four instead of reaching an agreement with Israel. Since August 1970 and particularly after the Egyptian violation of the ninety-day truce agreement in the Suez zone, United States interest in the four-power talks has cooled.

VIII

NASSER
LEAPFROGS
BAGHDAD
PACT

In the two-hour meeting in July 1955 in the Egyptian leader's home outside of Cairo, I had expected the dialogue to revolve mainly around the issues of the Israelis, whom he accused of flagrant aggression in Gaza, and around the United States failure to supply Egypt with major arms. But when Nasser launched into a blatant attack on the United States for collusion in inaugurating the Baghdad Pact, it was clear that the principal bone in his throat was not Ben-Gurion of Israel, but Nūri Said of Iraq.

"How dare the United States build a pact among Arab countries and omit Egypt, the most powerful nation in the Middle East?" he raged. In my efforts to placate him I said; "My country is fully aware of the importance of Egypt in the area, and there is no intention of bypassing your country. The pact is aimed at an Eastern power." He interrupted and asked me if I knew "if there was a worse bandit in the

Middle East than Nūri Said, the prime minister of Iraq."
I said I didn't know any. It was then that he announced with
a toss of his hand that he "would see in good time that
Nūri was disposed of."

Iraq, under Nūri Said's veteran hand, was the cornerstone
around which British-American policy in the Middle East
was to link the Arab world to the "Northern Tier" which
became known as the Baghdad Pact, the last resort of
England's fading hopes in the Middle East. The states form-
ing this "Northern Tier," closer to Russia and more fearful
of aggression, would be forged into a regional defense
organization. This was the origin of the Baghdad Pact, later
the Central Treaty Organization (CENTO). The pact was
initiated by a bilateral treaty between Turkey and Iraq, later
joined by Iran, Pakistan and Britain. It excluded Egypt and
also Israel. This was the pact that triggered Nasser's violent
opposition—"the last straw in his patience," causing the
schism between Egypt, the British, and the United States,
which sped Nasser's game of playing Soviet Russia against
the United States. It also led to the assassination of Nūri Said.

Nasser had consistently opposed the idea of an Arab pact
with the West, although he was willing to accept defensive
arrangements between non-Arab Middle Eastern states and
the West. On April 13, 1954, shortly after the announcement
of the Turkey-Pakistan pact, Nasser declared that Egypt
would oppose any attempt to bring Iraq into it on the
grounds that Nūri Said would deliberately weaken Arab
support for Egypt in her struggle against the British occupation of the Suez Canal zone.

Nasser had reason to detest and fear the veteran Iraqi
politician. While fearing Soviet support of the Kurdish

rebellious minority in northern Iraq, Nūri felt that the new alliance and the aid to follow would strengthen King Faisal's Iraqi monarchy and place him in that position of leadership in the Arab world which Nasser coveted. The pact served to revive and deepen the ancient hostility between the Nile and the Euphrates River civilizations.

The rivalry between Cairo and Baghdad had kept the Arab League ineffectual since its birth and had made a mockery of all the bombast about Arab unity. This goes back thousands of years to ancient historical conflicts that arose between the people of the Nile River and Euphrates River. The wounds never healed. The armies of the warring riparian civilizations have clashed many times in the general area of Palestine and the eastern Mediterranean.

The year 1953 was a crucial political turning point in the Middle East. A new revolutionary regime under Abdel Gamal Nasser had replaced the decadent Farouk regime in Egypt. The founding meeting of the Bandung Conference "third world" neutralist bloc had just been held. It was the start of a new ferment in the Arab world. The ideals of a new Arab generation were beginning to clash with older traditionalists in key Arab nations who had dominated Arab politics since the end of the World War I. A new crop of leaders was beginning to demand the riddance of old humili-ations that had wounded Arab dignity, especially between the two wars.

The revolutionary Arab world saw and began to work for the elimination from their midst of what they termed the last remnants of imperialism—the British bases in Egypt and French rule in Algiers and the countries of North Africa. Their old enmity toward Zionism and the Jewish independence movement, which had culminated in the establishment of Israel, led them to regard the State of Israel as part of this "imperialism." Out of the artificial division of the nations in the area imposed by outside powers after World War I, a single strong Pan-Arab bloc loomed as a possibility and became the gleam in the eye of Abdel Gamal Nasser, who saw himself as the leader of a coalition of Arab states into one United Arab Republic. Nasser himself was astonishingly frank about his power objectives. In his *The Philosophy of a Revolution,* he describes the "role in search of a hero"— the part for which he offered himself. The first of the "three circles" to be forged with Egypt as its center, and himself as the focus of that center, was the "Arab Circle." The others were to be the continent of Africa, and finally the entire Moslem world which, with megalomaniac immodesty, he enumerated as including his eighty million fellow Moslems in China, Indonesia, Pakistan, Malaya, Siam and Burma, as well as the forty million Moslems in the Soviet Union.

The extent to which Nasser had already made use of the African circle for the benefit of the Soviet Union was revealed by the Nigerian Government, when they credited the Soviet Union with major foreign aid. Nasser sent his Egyptian pilots to fly Soviet-built MIGs into Nigeria against Biafra.

United States policy toward this rising Arab nationalism was at first not hostile. Few tears were shed about the overthrow of King Farouk. The United States hoped to make the new Egyptian regime a valuable ally, and therefore encouraged Britain to evacuate the Suez Canal in a new treaty in 1954.

But British Prime Minister Anthony Eden and Secretary Dulles, concerned over possible Soviet aggression, decided that a regional defense organization must be formed to build a ring around Russia to block its progress of encroachment into the Middle East. This was not the first time that Western leaders had sought to organize the Arab states into a group to be used for Western security purposes. It was Eden who, as British foreign minister, in 1944, succeeded in promoting a meeting held in Alexandria at which the Arab League was born. But that organization was successful only in increasing Arab hostility toward the Jews of Palestine and later toward Israel.

Ten years later, however, Secretary Dulles was hoping for a pact in the Middle East that would complete the missing link between NATO in the West and SEATO in the Far East in the strategy of containment against the spread of Communist influence. Following a tour of the region in 1952, the first visit to the area by an American secretary of state, Dulles said: "The pact should be designed to grow from within out of a sense of common danger and common destiny."

The Western efforts to build up an anti-Soviet alliance along Russia's southern borders was watched closely in Moscow. Fully aware of the ancient enmity between Nasser and Nūri Said, the Russians further recalled the Arab proverb about friends and enemies. Nasser's growing impatience with the West was a means of turning the situation to their own advantage. Immediately upon Turkey's and Iraq's initial signatures on the Baghdad Pact, Nasser had launched a campaign designed to prevent any other Arab state from joining in. In April 1955, Russia addressed a note to all Middle East states warning them against joining the Pact and set about wooing Egypt. A trade agreement was signed between

Moscow and Cairo in August 1955; a similar trade agreement was signed between Cairo and Peking that same month, followed by other agreements with almost all the countries of the Eastern bloc. Within weeks, arms deliveries began to pour into Egypt, at first from Czechoslovakia. With them came the vanguard of the thousands of Russian military and economic technicians who were to follow.

Nasser's arms deal with the Soviet Union came as a stunning shock to Washington, but caused jubilation throughout the Arab world. It was the first successful defiance of Western tutelage by an Arab leader. Nasser felt he could now afford to play off one side of the cold war against the other for his own benefit. Secretary Dulles, increasingly unhappy about the turn of events in Russia's favor, expressed his astonishment: "We were appalled to discover that Nasser had become involved in an extensive deal to purchase more than $250 millions in airplanes, tanks, and other military equipment from the Soviet Union and Czechoslovakia, and had mortgaged Egypt's stockpile of cotton in payment."

Although the initial sale of more than $250 millions of Eastern bloc arms was, in retrospect, a relatively insignificant amount, the Russians were beginning to secure a means of countering Western containment. However small this initial Soviet entry into the area, the United States saw this Soviet-Egyptian relationship as the beginning of a Kremlin breakthrough. United States concern was further aggravated by Nasser's recognition of the Communist regime in Peking in May 1956.

However innocent of aggressive intent the Baghdad Pact may have seemed to its members and their allies, no Russian strategist worth his keep could help but interpret it as a network for potentially offensive missile bases against the Soviet mainland and Russia's sensitivity toward any threat to the integrity of its own security belt, the *cordon sanitaire*. At best it was a definite Western defense commitment that sharply restricted Russia's freedom of action in dealing with near-neighboring states to the south.

The sudden offer of Czech and Russian arms and Egypt's immediate response came therefore almost as a gift from heaven, a vehicle that offered a safe way to outflank the Baghdad Pact.

But more violent means were at hand. On July 14, 1958, the pro-American government of Iraq was overthrown in a bloody arms revolution led by General Kassim and cheered on by Nasser. King Faisal and Prime Minister Nūri Said were hunted down and murdered. As I read the reports of the dragging of the corpses of the King and his prime minister through the streets of Baghdad before cheering crowds, the echoes of Nasser's prediction made in his living room three years before echoed in my ears.

The overthrow of King Faisal and Nūri Said brought down the whole edifice of Western policy in that part of the Arab world and opened up a new range of opportunities that the Soviet Union was quick to exploit. Russia immediately announced its support of the new revolutionary regime of Kassim in Baghdad, offered arms and economic aid, and began warning outside powers not to interfere.

Iraq's fall was but a culmination of an interacting chain of events that had begun a political tug of war between the Russians and the West for domination of the Middle East. Dulles' fever against Nasser for his activities against the

Baghdad Pact had been rising after the arms deal with the Russians and jumped a few more points when Nasser recognized Red China.

In July 1956 the United States withdrew its offer to help finance the Aswân High Dam on the Nile (as precipitately as she had made it six months earlier) and persuaded Great Britain and the World Bank to do likewise.

Secretary Dulles' abrupt reversal of United States support for the Aswân Dam came after many months of study and negotiations with the Egyptians on the 1.3-billion-dollar project which had the sponsorship of Eugene Black, president of the World Bank, who described it as "the largest single structure ever undertaken in the history of the world." Dulles' reversal was like a punch in the stomach to Nasser.

Nasser and Nehru were airborne when the news of Dulles' decision flashed around the world. They were returning on July 19 from a visit with Tito on the Yugoslav island of Brioni and only at the Cairo Airport at 2 A.M. was the grim news broken to Nasser. His reaction was volcanic.

Nasser had been playing off the United States' bids for the financing and building of the dam against Russia's. Now he was left with only one great power to deal with, which at the moment was increasingly preoccupied with riots in Poland and a full-scale revolt brewing in Hungary. Nevertheless, on the day following Dulles' announcement, Ambassador Kiselev in Cairo said that he felt sure Russia would keep her promise to finance the Aswân Dam if Egypt should request it. But the Russians were slow on the uptake and only made their offer of aid for the Aswân Dam two years later, in 1958.

The arms deals with Czechoslovakia and the USSR had brought with them to Egypt the first of a steady procession of Russian experts in the military field. The agreement for Soviet financial and technical aid in building the Aswân Dam was to lead to the large-scale influx into Egypt of other Russian experts. While overseeing construction work on the dam and the installation of electric-power systems throughout Egypt, they were also in a position to strengthen the Russian presence within Egypt in all fields of economic and political life.

America's withdrawal from the Aswân Dam project did not mean the end of American financial aid to Egypt, though Nasser had a tendency to gloss this over. The United States record shows outright gifts of more than one billion dollars' worth of credits (food, etc.) to Egypt between 1953 and 1966. Only when Washington finally saw that the Egyptian leader's game of blackmailing the United States against Russian threats was not paying off was the American handout halted.

Nasser himself has credited Nehru of India and President Tito of Yugoslavia with teaching him the game of extracting funds by playing the Russians against the Americans. It was at the Bandung Conference that Nasser was admitted to the "club" which qualified him for the Big League euchering of major finances from the big powers. Whoever the teacher, Nasser proved to be more than an apt pupil. His performance in extracting funds so prodigious from both Moscow and Washington was great enough to have earned him during his lifetime the championship title of "international fund raiser" of modern times.

IX

SWALLOWING
NASSER'S
"LINE"

I had arrived in Cairo in July 1955 for the clandestine meeting with Colonel Nasser, at a time when the Middle East
crisis was working up to a new climax. Nasser's response to
my concern about the danger of an explosion was to launch
into a bitter attack on the Israelis, whom he accused of
initiating hostilities. When I suggested a moratorium, a
cooling-off period, he said: "It would be next to impossible
to enforce. How many spies do you think we have in
Israel?" he queried. I hestitated to guess. "Two thousand,"
was his punctuated reply, "and I have no doubt that the
Israelis have at least that many in Egypt. Spies are instructed, if caught, to shoot. How can both of our countries
get instructions to them during such a period? It doesn't
seem possible." The Arabs whom Nasser referred to as his
"spies" were actually the Fedayeen terrorists sent at night

into Israel partly to gather intelligence but mainly to lay mines and harass Israeli farmers.

But I pressed on: "There must be something we can agree on," I insisted. "Some small point, a basis to begin with in negotiations."

"What, for instance?" he asked.

"Perhaps," I said, "we can agree on our mutual imperfections." From this I got the only smile, albeit a wry one, from the handsome Egyptian leader in my entire two-hour meeting. Nasser finally agreed to accept me as a liaison for possible future discussions but warned me, on the way out of his suburban home, that I would get nowhere with Ben-Gurion.

My meeting with Nasser had been arranged outside diplomatic channels. The American Ambassador, Henry A. Byroade, was *persona non grata* with Nasser at the time. My close friend Arthur Hays Sulzberger, the publisher of *The New York Times,* had sent a message to his correspondent in Cairo, Kennett Love, to help me. I found Love and his attractive young wife, Felicity, with a brood of children, a devoted friend of Nasser. It was he who arranged the surreptitious appointment for me with the Egyptian leader at his home outside Cairo.

Love had fallen completely for the Nasser line. In a heated debate over Egypt's policy that lasted until the early hours of the morning at Mena House, we watched the moon seem to bend down over the pyramids and the Sphinx. But there was nothing sphinxlike about Love's approach in his stories filed back to the *Times.* Their prejudice in favor of Nasser and his regime was almost transparent. In introducing me to the Egyptian leader, Love was hoping that I, too, would become captive of the charisma and persuasive talents of Nasser and become a convert to his philosophy to take back to America and to his publisher. To have turned an ardent advocate of the democracy of Israel into a sympathizer of the Nasser line would have been a priceless feather in his cap. Love should have known better. A less naïve and youthful enthusiastic captive of the Egyptian's personality would have been more realistic in appraising the unbending commitment to continue my service to the people of Israel in their rightful aims of survival as a democracy. Yet, I shall always be grateful for the door Love opened for the face-to-face confrontation with the late enigmatic, dynamic Egyptian dictator.

During my stay in Cairo I was aware of secret meetings that were being held between the Israelis and the Egyptians under the United Nations auspices of General Burns. The site of the meetings was a tent in the desert on a line separating the two countries. Joseph Tekoah, Israel's present ambassador to the United Nations, and Salah Gohar were the two representatives of their countries.

When I arrived in Israel, via Cyprus, General Burns invited me to a private dinner at Government House in "No Man's Land" on the outskirts of Jerusalem, ominously enough on the Biblical "Hill of Evil Council." During dinner Burns reported his frustration from the dead center on which his meetings between the Israelis and the Egyptians had been impaled. "We are stalled. We cannot even get agreement on an agenda," he complained.

"Why not start the talks without an agenda?" I suggested—an idea so simple it seemed not to have occurred to anyone.

The next day in Jerusalem I was awakened early by an

urgent telephone call from Harry Gilroy, correspondent in Israel of the *Times,* who also had a message from Arthur Sulzberger to help me.

A story had appeared on the front page of *The New York Times* under Love's by-line, reporting that it was heard in Cairo that Burns was about to be replaced by the United Nations Secretariat. This obviously was sparked by Love's Egyptian friends following the General's cables of April 6 and 8, reporting that the mounting border forays had been instigated by Nasser's Fedayeen commandos.

Abdul Kadar Hatem, Egypt's director of information, who had accompanied me on my visit with Nasser, had broadly hinted to me that *The New York Times* could be a "useful friend" to Egypt. Love, it turned out, had become a *priceless* friend of Egypt at the expense of accurate reporting.

I invited Burns to meet me at the King David Hotel in Jerusalem. Despite the story's exclusively journalistic origin, he was visibly shaken by imputations that discredited him. In response to an urgent cable to my friend Ralph Bunche, deputy to Dag Hammarskjöld at the United Nations, Burns received a prompt message from the Secretariat reassuring him of its complete support of his work and position.

On returning to Cairo, I flatly accused Love of "loading" his story, stating that it was designed to get Burns fired. Love denied it. His distinctly pro-Egypt bias was due, I concluded, in part at least to his total ignorance of what was going on in Israel just forty miles to the east. To a degree, the same could be said of Harry Gilroy, who, from his view in Jerusalem, could see only the virtues of Israel. Through the United States diplomatic pouch I rushed a note to Arthur Sulzberger suggesting that it would be a service to the *Times'* readers if Love and Gilroy were to swap positions. Each would get an "education" in the opposition country that would provide more objective reporting. Sulzberger promptly accepted my suggestion.

The exchange of these two ace reporters took place with a ceremony at the Mandelbaum Gate, which separated Jordan from Israel. But in their newly assigned capitals both men met with finely honed hostility based on their past performances in opposite capitals. After a few months, both were reassigned to other posts far removed from the Middle East. Love, a talented and hard-working reporter, left the journalistic field, but his attachment to the Nasser regime never left him. In 1969 he wrote a book, a strident apologia for Nasser and a fierce diatribe against Israel. In this massive book, Love's complete lack of objectivity as I witnessed it in Cairo is nothing more than an extension of his adoration of Nasser, a voluminous transparent propaganda tract for Nasser and his regime.

I listened on the radio from Cairo to increasingly bombastic public statements (translated for me from the Arabic), threatening to extinguish Israel and throw its people into the sea. My friends in the Department of State urged me not to take these seriously, as they were "empty rhetoric" intended only for "Arab consumption." I disagreed. My observations, confirmed by the bitter experience of the Israelis, did not allow me to swallow this line. What I heard Nasser telling his people in Egypt is what he intended doing. It was his suave, smiling, persuasive talk in interviews with me and editors of mass-circulation American magazines and with TV interviewers which were intended to cajole and mislead.

In fact, Nasser's publicly expressed threats against Israel call for no theoretical interpretation. They were backed up by Fedayeen terrorist action that he had ordered. Following his seizure of the Suez Canal, his prestige in the Arab world skyrocketed. There were enough indications that the Egyptian ruler was now feeling confident of his ability to launch an all-out attack against Israel by his Arab Confederate States.

X

"THE
BEAR
IS USING
NASSER"

In a single week in July 1956, events crowded with such dramatic and climactic impact as to change the history of the Middle East and shake the world.

On July 19, Secretary Dulles abruptly withdrew the United States offer to finance the Aswân High Dam. Three days later, July 22, the anniversary of the Egyptian revolution, Nasser decided what his answer to Dulles would be and outlined it to his close associates. Plans that had been gestating long before now found the hour of birth.

On July 26, before a crowd in Alexandria estimated at a quarter million, Nasser announced that he had nationalized the Suez Canal. To an almost unbroken din of clapping and cheering, he shouted: "Today, O citizens, with the annual income of the Suez Canal amounting to one hundred million dollars a year, five hundred million dollars in five years, we shall not look for the seventy million dollars of American aid . . . and whenever any talk comes from Washington, I shall tell them: 'Drop dead of your fury.' "* The world was stunned.

Nasser's facile, unrealistic arithmetic for the dam's payment turned out to be one of his most flamboyant flights into financial fantasy. Billions, not millions, of dollars were needed to build the dam. Nor could the hysterical mob in Alexandria realize that the dammed waters with their gradual and graduated flow for year-round irrigation, plus the vast quantities of electric power to be generated, would not bring them the economic paradise they had been promised. Much of the benefit from this vast project would be offset by Egypt's explosive birth rate. At best, the Egyptian peasant and the Egyptian economy would only be able to mark time, without slipping further backwards, as long as Egypt's leader continued to squander billions on armaments and barter Egypt's hard-currency earnings from its cotton crop for guns from Russia.

But it was a time of worry in world capitals as nearly every country traded through the Suez Canal in its own or in other countries' ships.

Nasser's seizure threatened to cut off Europe's lifeline. Oil was that lifeline. Any interruption in its regular flow meant virtual suffocation of the European economy.

I was in Paris in December 1956. While in New York I had only an academic reading acquaintance with the blockage. Abroad, it became a frightening reality. The Suez war had blockaded all shipments of oil to Europe. In Paris I beheld the unbelievable spectacle of watching all traffic in the French capital at a virtual standstill.

* BBC Summary of World Broadcasts.

Here was a rehearsal—convincing advance proof of how the exercise of power control over Western Europe would work—a lesson not lost on the Russians.

The news of the Suez seizure was brought to British Prime Minister Anthony Eden while he was entertaining at dinner young King Faisal of Iraq and the Iraqi Premier Nūri Said. Within an hour Eden had summoned a meeting of the British cabinet. In the House of Commons the following day, Eden declared that Britain could not tolerate "Nasser's thumb on our windpipe."

The next day a cable was delivered to President Eisenhower from Eden in which the British leader said: "If we take a firm stand over this now we shall have the support of all maritime powers. If we do not, our influence and yours throughout the Middle East will, we are all convinced, be finally destroyed."* History was to show the accuracy of this forecast. As we shall see later, it was Secretary of State Dulles who was to block the "firm action" planned by Eden.

Eisenhower sent the veteran troubleshooter Robert Murphy to London with instructions to find out if the British and French would go to war. Murphy's cable home was to the effect that London and Paris were, indeed, planning to fight to prevent Nasser from strangling their economies.

It was clear that Eden and the French were much more concerned about the consequences of Nasser's coup than was Dulles, who was involving himself with matters closer to home, such as the forthcoming presidential election. A year earlier he had expressed the opinion that United States

* Sir Anthony Eden, *Full Circle: Memoirs.* Cambridge, Mass., 1960, p. 476.

policies had finally "contained" the Russians and that the *Communist diplomatic offensive was on the retreat.* The inventor of "brinkmanship" in international politics, he now found the tables being turned by Nasser on Britain and France. But war was something else. Military action against Egypt might lead to Soviet intervention, which would inevitably draw the United States into hostilities. Dulles began to have doubts about his earlier certainty that he had foxed Moscow.

The relationship between Dulles and Eden was of mutual dislike bordering on detestation. Early in 1952, Eden had appealed privately to Eisenhower *not* to appoint Dulles secretary of state if he were elected. This appeal was due to an earlier disagreement between Dulles and Britain's Herbert Morrison, in which the Englishman had accused Dulles of misleading Britain on Japanese recognition of Chiang Kai-shek. Informed privately by Eisenhower of his intention to appoint Dulles secretary of state, Eden confided to Eisenhower: "I do not think I would be able to work with him again."* And yet it was these two men who were now called upon to act jointly in answering Nasser's seizure of Suez.

For Dulles, the way to avoid a war was to call a conference. Eden's first mistake in the unhappy history of the Suez affair was to agree to Dulles' proposal for a conference rather than to pursue unrelentingly the Anglo-French decision of a show of force.

Dulles had internationalized the dispute by making the British and French accept a relatively broad-based con-

* Roscoe Drummond and Gaston Coblentz, *Duel at the Brink.* New York, 1960, p. 165.

ference, and he had thereby slowed down their plans for war. In fact, the main reason hostilities had not already begun was that neither Great Britain nor France was ready. "Had they done it quickly," Eisenhower said later, "we would have accepted it." Eden answered critics of his delay by saying: "We had nothing like enough airborne troops for an operation of this kind." Without enough paratroopers, the invasion had to be launched from Malta, a thousand miles east of Egypt, and the service chiefs had told Eden that they would not be ready before six months.

Eden wrote bitterly: "In practice it was to mean conferences and resolution, but no action. The result was words." It was undoubtedly one of the wordiest of crises even for the Middle East; but words did not prevent Eden from completing his war preparations.

Anthony Eden built his vendetta against one man, the leader of Egypt. In a BBC broadcast, which was carried on Britain's and four major United States networks, he said: "Our quarrel is not with Egypt, still less with the Arab world, it is with Colonel Nasser." Secretary Dulles, alarmed at Britain's unbending intention of going to war, gradually pulled away from associating the United States with the British and French punitive position. Eden's cable to President Eisenhower on August 23, following the failure of the conference to agree on a compromise, is almost prescient in the light of Russia's progressive steps toward her goal in the Middle East.

The Bear is using Nasser, with or without his knowledge . . . first to dislodge the West from the Middle East, and second to get a foothold in Africa so as to dominate that continent in turn. . . . We have many friends in the Middle East and in Africa . . . but they will not be strong enough to stand against the power of the mobs if Nasser wins again. The firmer the front we show together, the greater the chance that Nasser will give way without the need for any resort to force.

The second plan worked out by Dulles called for the establishment of a "Suez Canal Users' Association," but it did not have enough teeth in it even to approach success.

Meanwhile, Eisenhower was entering the final phases of the election campaign for a second term as President. The former commander in chief of the Allied forces in Europe in World War II appeared before the people as a man of peace who was opposed to the warlike intentions of his former comrades-in-arms. The Suez Canal was deftly muted as a campaign issue. Vice-President Nixon played only a small part in the Suez affair—he was busy politicking.

A campaign speech Nixon made after the Suez war on November 2 to answer criticism of the Administration's Mideastern policy (written in part by Dulles) included:

"This vote [for the cease-fire ordered by the General Assembly] constituted a worldwide vote of confidence, the like of which has never been known before. It is significant that only five opposed our resolution. . . .

In the past, the nations of Asia and Africa have always felt we would, when the pressure was on, side with the policies of the British and French governments in relation to the once colonial areas. . . .

For the first time in history we have shown independence of Anglo-French policies toward Asia and Africa which seemed to us to reflect the colonial tradition. That declaration of independence has had an electrifying effect throughout the world.

Nixon made another speech on December 6 (also largely written by Dulles). It was delivered to prepare the ground for Dulles' appearance at a NATO meeting four days later, where he was to discuss the question of consultation among the allies. It was a hymn of praise for Eisenhower and Dulles, and was full of inaccuracies.

Referring to the "great events of the last forty days," Nixon said:

> Lesser men would have sought easy vote-getting solutions on the eve of an election. They [Eisenhower and Dulles] chose statesmanship and high moral principles. . . . With regard to our alliances, it is essential that we recognize that history may record that neither we nor our allies were without fault in our handling of the events which led to the crisis in which we now find ourselves. Our friends believe that we did not appreciate adequately the provocation which brought about their action and that we did not assume our proper responsibility in working out a settlement of the basic problem existing in that area. . . .
>
> We, on the other hand, felt that we had some legitimate criticisms to make of their policies during this period.

Across the Atlantic, passions were running high. Eden distrusted Dulles' legalistic approach and deliberate vacillation. The United Nations Security Council was powerless to act in the face of Nasser's intransigence and Russia's veto power. The result was that both England and France stepped up their military plans for war to recover the Suez Canal. As for Eden, he wrote grimly in his memoirs:

I soon learnt that the Soviet Government regarded the proceedings at the UN as a victory for Egypt and for them. In this way they were undoubtedly right. I was not surprised when messages from our friends in the Middle East showed dismay at Nasser's swelling success.

XI

ISRAEL
REACTS

For Israel, Nasser's seizure of the Suez Canal had little effect. Even under the Suez Canal Company, the canal had been closed to the ships of Israel and to cargoes aboard foreign ships bound to and from Israel. As his excuse for his blockade of the waterway (already twice declared illegal by the United Nations Security Council, but maintained nevertheless), Nasser cited the fact that he was in a "state of war" with Israel. Yet, when Israel's retaliatory actions against Egyptian attacks were discussed at the United Nations, Egypt claimed that "no state of war exists" and was invariably backed up by the Russians and the Eastern block.

The Egyptian ban on the passage of the ships of Israel was not only carried out in disregard of Security Council resolutions; it was also expressly barred by the terms of the

Israeli-Egyptian armistice agreement of 1949, which forbade hostile activities between the parties.

But the Suez blockade was not the only hostile activity carried out in breach of the agreement. Defeated on the battlefield, Colonel Nasser sought to pursue an undeclared war by the infiltration of his armies across Israel's borders on terrorist raids. Recourse to the United Nations Security Council proved useless, as the Soviet Union was ever ready to cast its veto to block the slightest condemnation of its Egyptian client. Israel, however, was invariably condemned for retaliation against the repeated attacks.

In 1955, the year of the first Soviet-Egyptian arms deal, Nasser began the organization of the Fedayeen, the guerrilla army of Egyptian-trained and equipped Palestinian refugees, bent on the destruction of Israel.

The danger to Mideastern peace represented by these terrorist activities was fully understood by the United Nations' chief truce supervisor, General E. L. M. Burns, who reported to Secretary General U Thant on April 8, 1956:

> I am dispatching to the foreign minister of Egypt a protest against the action of the Fedayeen, assuming it to have been authorized or tolerated by the Egyptian authorities, and requesting immediate withdrawal of any persons under Egyptian control from the territory of Israel.
>
> This follows my attempt on April 6 to get an assurance that the Egyptian authorities were not contemplating allowing these terrorists to infiltrate into Israel. . . . I consider that if Egypt has ordered these Fedayeen raids she has now put herself in the position of an aggressor.

Nasser's reply, on April 21, 1956, was to establish a joint military command of Egypt, Syria, Saudi Arabia, and

Yemen, under Egyptian command, aimed at Israel. Eight days later Cairo Radio announced that Fedayeen commanders in Egypt, Jordan, Syria, and Lebanon had met to organize a concerted campaign against Israel.

As the year progressed with futile London conferences to retrieve the Suez Canal, Egyptian Fedayeen aggression against Israel mounted. Questioned in September 1956 about terrorist activity at one of his frequent press conferences, Dulles replied suavely that he "deplored" and "regretted" the outbreak of additional border incidents, adding: "At the moment I do not see any likelihood of a direct relationship of this situation to the Suez Canal situation. Conceivably, one might develop, but so far the two issues have been rather independent of each other."

If the two issues had been independent of each other, this situation was not to last long. While the British and French were still arguing with Dulles in the summer of 1956 about action against Nasser's seizure of the canal, General Moshe Dayan, then Israeli chief of staff (and present minister of defense) flew secretly to Paris on September 28 to discuss further arms purchases to counter the flow of Soviet arms to Egypt. The government of Israel had had secret information from Paris on September 1 concerning the Anglo-French plan (the code was named "Musketeers") to mount an attack to seize the Suez Canal and return it to international control until its original charter ran out. On the assumption that the plan would be put in motion, Israel could not fail to make its own military preparation to ensure passage for Israeli ships through the international waterway and to put an end—once and for all—to terrorist activities directed from

Egypt. If the Anglo-French invasion plan were not to take place, Israel would have to act alone.

At the time, representatives of world chancelleries at the United Nations in New York, not especially friendly to Israel and abhorring the possibility of war in the area, were quite frank in confessing to me that "Israel must either break out of the siege closing tighter around it or be destroyed."

Marauding across the borders from both Jordan and the Egyptian Gaza Strip was taking an increasing death toll as the year 1956 progressed. Israeli retaliation was quick and fierce. Meanwhile, at the first operational meeting at which plans for the Sinai campaign were drawn up, the question of possible Soviet intervention was raised. Dayan noted in his diary:

> The shorter the campaign, the greater the chances that no new volunteers will come; if they do come, they are likely to be Czechs or Poles, but not Russians; such "volunteers" are likely to be not infantry units or tank crews, but pilots, so that we shall meet them only in the air. I have no doubt that this will be less pleasant than facing Egyptian pilots.

This was the first time that the danger of Soviet involvement had to be faced by Israel. This attitude of awareness and readiness which has persisted to this day may have served to help moderate Soviet aggressive plans for attack later. Even with full knowledge that the results would be a walkover for the Russians, it was obvious that Moscow did not relish a show of force, even against a minor power, that might bring one or more of the Western powers into a major conflict.

In early 1970, when news first trickled out that Soviet pilots were flying operational missions with the Egyptian air force, the Russians, apparently heeding Dayan's warning that Israel would not shrink from an aerial confrontation over the Suez Canal, carefully kept behind the battle line twenty miles west of the canal. This was the zone in which the Israelis declared the Russians would not be permitted to operate. Nevertheless, the Russians moved their SAM III missiles within twelve miles of the Suez in direct violation of the ninety-day truce of August 1970. The implications behind the Russian show of contempt for an agreement with the United States cannot be overestimated.

While Israel would not shrink from a clash with Soviet pilots, it was up to the United States to warn off the Russians from further dangerous escalation of the crisis which elevated it from a regional Middle East clash to an East-West confrontation not only of Russian and American-built aircraft but also of soldiers of the East and West camps.

XII

POLITICAL
VICTORY
FOR THE
MOSCOW-CAIRO
AXIS

Washington during those critical days of the summer and autumn of 1956 suffered a dense blackout of diplomatic news from England and France. The Department of State had no news whatsoever from across the Atlantic, while United States intelligence reported heavily increased coded communications between Israel and Paris. But the code was not broken, and with war brewing Dulles was kept completely in the dark. For this secrecy toward the United States, Dulles could never forgive his allies. He could not have realized that it was his own devious and legalistic tactics of obfuscation and vacillation that finally forced the British and French to take action alone and to exclude further American delaying tactics.

The reaction of Dulles to the British and French assault, according to one State Department official, was "close to apoplexy." He sent for Hervé Alphand, the French Ambassador, and, his face flushed with anger, he said: "This is the darkest day in the history of the Western Alliance. It might even be the end of the alliance itself . . . the news blackout has done me the gravest personal damage and has put me in an impossible situation . . . the action and intervention of France and Britain is just the same as the behavior of the Soviet Union in Budapest." Alphand protested vigorously and Dulles realized he had gone too far. "I withdraw the comparison," he said. "I beg your pardon. You must understand I am speaking under the stress of the great emotion that such a terrible thing could have happened."

To relatives and associates Dulles said: "How could people do this to *me*?" "How could they pull a stunt like this on me when I've been working with them all these weeks? They seemed to accept my lead all along."

White House and State Department aides revealed later, while thinking back over those days of crisis, that both Eisenhower and Dulles lost their heads when the news of the Israeli move into Sinai and of the Anglo-French invasion came through. Claiming that they had been "flouted" and "betrayed," they appear to have lost their grip. Their personal resentment and personal vindictiveness were allowed to overcome their cool judgment. When Dulles heard of the Israeli invasion, his face and neck were flushed with anger as he immediately called a staff conference. As for the President, when he heard of the military activities of the three countries, "the White House rang with barracks-room language that had not been heard at 1600 Pennsylvania Avenue since the days of General Grant," according to one aide.

The loss of control was to pluck Nasser from defeat and hand a victory to the Soviet Union that Moscow had never anticipated.

Unfortunately, the French and British military operation had been clumsy and inept. The two great powers put on a so surprisingly amateurish military show in their movement of troops to the battle zone that it cost them the war. The opposite proved true of the Israeli operation. They sliced across the Sinai and within twenty-four hours all their military objectives and more were met according to plan.

But they were not permitted to keep their victory. Moscow expediently played on the weakness and fright that suddenly overcame Dulles and Eisenhower. The Kremlin's missile threats blew a chill of almost paralytic fear through Washington. Along with the incredible bungling of the British and French, Israel found itself surrounded by an atmosphere of failure instead of a climate of victory that it had alone achieved in its military push.

If the combined political pressure from the newly improvised partnership of Washington and Moscow was too much for England and France to stand up against, Israel could certainly not be expected to resist alone. Reluctantly she withdrew her forces from the Sinai Peninsula which she had taken so quickly. Israel, however, learned a lesson that was to stand her in good stead. Her firm stance since June 1967 and her insistence on negotiation with her Arab neighbors before any ground is again given up can be traced back to the costly lessons learned in 1956.

Israel was not the only one to learn from the experience of those tremulous weeks. A year later, shortly before his death in 1957, Dulles hinted in confidence to an Israeli diplomat that if he had to go through the Suez Canal–Sinai experience again he would act differently this time.

In the light of Russia's later backdown following her missile threat in Cuba in 1962 when President Kennedy stood firm, it seems evident that the Russians would have backed down in 1956 had Khrushchev's bluff been called by Eisenhower and Dulles.

The Russians lost no time in throwing their full weight behind the Security Council debates to save Nasser's prestige from his debacle. The temporary alliance of Washington and Moscow won back for Egypt everything that had been lost on the battlefield. The Suez Canal remained in Nasser's hands. The two billion dollars in war matériel lost to the Israelis was speedily replaced by the Soviets. Nasser had been lifted back on his horse by the joint Soviet-American hoist.

Thanks to Eisenhower and Dulles the Suez operation resulted in a powerful gain for Moscow. With the Suez Canal now firmly in Nasser's hands, he returned to his threatening posture against the Israelis, although even more firmly in the debt of his patron, the Kremlin. As for the British and French, they were completely knocked out of the Middle East. One lesson, however, was learned by them from the abortive Suez campaign. Their dependence on their oil economics demanded that they construct giant supertankers to carry oil more cheaply around the Cape of Good Hope instead of through the Suez Canal in smaller ships.

For the Israelis the lessons were hard and manifold. The deep wounds of the Suez war remained unhealed until the military victory of the Six-Day War of 1967. The most enduring lesson for them was, however, not to put their trust in vague promises of outside powers.

The Middle East was not the only area in that portentous autumn of 1956 where the lid blew off. During the boiling point in the Suez crisis, the Hungarian pressure cooker also steamed over with an incipient revolt against the Soviet masters. The American secretary of state was cocksure after the Budapest uprising. Dulles again saw the mirage of the monolith of Communism crumbling.

But fortified by his colossal successful bluff of Dulles and Eisenhower in forcing the British, French, and Israelis to back away from Suez, Khrushchev was in no mood to trifle with recalcitrant Hungarians. Soviet tanks quickly rolled through the streets of Budapest.

In two separate major international crises that autumn, the Russians had put the squeeze on Washington to find that they could send the greatest power on earth running for cover. Is there any wonder that the Soviets today, in dealing with the Israelis, who stubbornly refuse to commit suicide to satisfy the aims of any major or minor power, take encouragement from the precedent of 1956 to put pressure on President Nixon, who was a key member of the United States "team" that the Russians had been able to manipulate for the Kremlin's benefit.

RUSSIA CONSOLIDATES HER POSITION

XIII

THE
ROOTS
OF
TERRORISM

As I was entering a Hashemite Kingdom of Jordan airplane in Beirut for Amman in July 1969, I received a message from Ambassador Symmes in Jordan, urging that the visit be postponed. The terrorists in the Jordan capital had become so unruly that the embassy could not guarantee my safety.

The ambassador's caution proved to be more than justified. Some months later, as Joseph Sisco, Assistant Secretary of State, was about to leave for Amman, he received a similar signal in Jerusalem, and canceled his visit. Two days later, King Hussein declared Symmes *persona non grata* and the ambassador was obliged to vacate his post.

In June 1970, war broke out between the Arab terrorists and King Hussein's army, as it had in Lebanon some months previously between terrorists and the Lebanese gendarmerie. Seventy-four American citizens were locked up and kept as hostages for forty-eight hours in the Inter-Continental Hotel in Amman. The American military attaché was assassinated, and two of the wives of American officials were raped. The three-day battle which bordered on a civil war took seven hundred Arab lives, and Hussein's shaky throne came nearer to the verge of toppling.

This was a mere skirmish compared to the bloody civil war that swept the country in September of the same year when the terrorists, reinforced temporarily by Syrian artillery, came within hours of capturing Amman, over-running the monarchy, and setting the entire Middle East ablaze.

The trip to Amman would have been my third to the grown-up village in the hills of Moab which had become Jordan's capital. Before it was battered by civil war, Amman was a city of some attractiveness. It was built, like Rome, on seven hills, with its minarets and stone dwellings on cliffs. In 1960, as part of a study as consultant for the United Nations Relief and Works Administration (UNRWA), I spent a week in Jordan with Harry Howard, a Department of State representative for refugee matters. It was then that I met King Hussein at a reception given for him in the large open garden outside the home of United States Ambassador Sheldon T. Mills.

A cloak-and-dagger episode right out of Eric Ambler preceded the party. In the afternoon, a former Palestinian visited me in the office of the UNRWA headquarters and warned me not to attend the party for the king that night. Unabashedly, in a matter-of-fact voice, he said to me, "We intend to kill the king tonight. He is a man of many lives. We thought we had him a number of times, but he miraculously escaped. Tonight," he leaned across my desk and whispered, "we expect to get him. Don't get in the way of a bullet." I thanked him for his solicitude and reported the conversation to Ambassador Mills, who replied nonchalantly that such threats were common currency in Amman. The king's bodyguard and loyal cohort among the Bedouin had managed to act as a shield against the increasing belligerence of the refugees who had vacated Palestine in 1948 and who the king had made citizens of Jordan.

At the reception that night in the garden, I spoke only briefly to the king, who was surrounded by beautiful women. But I did manage informally, over a drink with his foreign minister, Hazza el-Majali, and the British ambassador, to bring up discreetly the subject of peace with Israel. Our conversation took a promising turn, and I felt that I had made an opening for future talks. The next day, Majali was killed in his office. A bomb exploded at a conference that the king was expected to attend.

On my second visit to Amman in 1965, I made a full day's trip up the Jordan River with young members of the Jordanian government to inspect the East Ghor Canal, built with United States Point 4 money. On the way up to the Lake of Galilee, I had plenty of time to talk informally with the young Jordanian engineers, all of whom had attended colleges in the United States. At noon, we stopped for "lunch" at a hostel, where I joined my hosts in a maladroit effort to appear casual by eating the lamb and rice with my right hand, Arab style. While we stood around a table in shirtsleeves, I decided to take advantage of the apparent spirit of camaraderie to introduce the touchy subject of peace with Israel. In a flash, as though a red flag had been raised in front of bulls, the atmosphere changed, and I became the target of invective from the Jordanians, whose unhappiness stemmed principally from their inability to make contact with their families who then resided in Israel. (Since the 1967 war they have joined their families, but the rising pressure of the Palestinians against Israel has not abated.)

At a turn of the Jordan that was so narrow we could have walked across the muddy river, I pointed into Israel and said to my host, "How ridiculous that this tiny waterway should separate two hardworking groups of farmers from living and working at peace with each other!" I was stopped in my tracks. "There will be no peace," they shot back abruptly. "We intend to get over there and take that land back from the Israelis," they cried with a defiant wave of the hand.

How could I have predicted that a few years later these young Jordanians, educated in the United States with U.S. funds, would become members of an avenging terrorist organization that would hijack passenger planes of international air lines, abducting and victimizing 550 passengers and hold them as hostages for three weeks under perilous conditions?

With typical *Arabian Nights* fantasy and exaggeration, the terrorist leaders have described the exploits of their followers in bombing supermarkets and school buses, a university cafeteria, and civilian aircraft as the actions of resistance fighters against superior military odds. Their tall tales and photogenic sheikh headgear have caught the imagination and camera lenses of Western journalists, but their threats to liquidate Israel and seek a military solution have placed Moscow in a dilemma: the Soviet Union talks about a "political solution" to the Middle East problem, while Arafat and his men are bent only on the military annihilation of Israel.

These modern fanciful tales of *A Thousand and One Nights* have their roots deep in the heritage of a people whose ancient glory has long since faded and who have since been suffering from a massive national inferiority complex. This has brought about a split personality of the people which defies a rational approach to reality, a resort to rhetoric of yesterday's glory as a substitute for today's reality.

They are like actors who, with light turned on them in front of the camera, assume that the rest of the stage is thrown into darkness. The modern descendants of people who kept alight the torch of learning while Europe slumbered through the Dark Ages, they now find themselves far and away behind those they had surpassed.

During the Middle Ages, when whatever learning there was in Europe was almost limited to prelates and monks, it was the people of the Moslem Empire around the Mediterranean who advanced the arts and sciences by their poetry and architecture, their innovations in mathematics and philosophy, and their discoveries in medicine and astronomy. Ironically, many of these thinkers and innovators were Jews* designated by their Arabic names. With the decline of the Arab empire, however, after their defeat and expulsion from Spain and southern France, the Arabs as a people seem to have fallen asleep. This was at the very time when Europe was about to experience the Renaissance and the Reforma-

---

* Maimonides (Muses ben Maimon: 1135–1204) was but one of hundreds of Jews who achieved fame and dignity under medieval Arab rulers.

tion, which brought about the modern flowering of the arts and sciences.

When the Arabs finally awoke again, as a people, with the rise of modern nationalism during the latter half of the nineteenth century and the first decades of the twentieth, the Arabs found that their ancient leadership had been lost. This discovery was to make them embittered, especially as they now were ruled by the "infidels" (non-Moslems) they had themselves despised.*

A Westerner who lived among the Arabs and knew them well, T. E. Lawrence (Lawrence of Arabia), summed up the political idea of Arab unity as a "madman's notion." Their ideal of national unity, he said, was "an episodic combined resistance to an invader." "Their thoughts," he wrote, "were at ease only in extremes. They inhabited superlatives by choice."

He went on: "They are a dogmatic people, despising

---

* Dr. Sania Hamady, an Arab social psychologist, writes: "The Arabs possess one striking characteristic: their reaction to failures and slurs is often offensive rather than defensive. This inclination seems to have been partially institutionalized and greatly affected by the traditional call of *dj*ihād!—the call for a Holy War undertaken by the dār al-harb—the 'war area' where Moslems are not in control. The idea of the *dj*ihād has not passed from the Arab world. Religious leaders still issue the call for holy war against the infidel, whether it be Zionist or Westerner who are both considered to be in the war area of the dār al-harb." (*Temperament and Character of the Arabs,* Twayne Publishers, New York.)

The Arabs have long had their own self-analysts. The 14th-century Arab historian Ibn Khaldun, examining the earlier Moslem empire and its failure, wrote: "Generally speaking, the Arabs are incapable of founding an empire, except on a religious basis such as the revelation of a prophet or a saint . . . because their fierce character, pride, roughness and jealousy of one another, especially in political matters, make them the most difficult of peoples to lead. . . . The Arabs are the least willing of nations to subordinate themselves to each other, as they are rude, proud, ambitious, and eager to be the leader."

doubt, our modern crown of thorns . . . they are a people of spasms, of upheavals."

A modern Arab historian, Edward Selim Atiyah, writes: "It is a characteristic of the Arab mind to be swayed more by words than by ideas, and more by ideas than by facts."

Dr. Sania Hamady, in *Temperament and Character of the Arabs,* notes: "Lying is a wide-spread habit among the Arabs, and they have a low idea of truth." She quotes the medieval Moslem theologian al-Ghazali: "Know that a lie is not wrong in itself, but only because of the evil conclusions to which it leads the hearer, making him believe something that is not really the case. . . . It is sometimes a duty to lie. . . . We must lie when truth leads to unpleasant results."

The Arabs, of course, are not the only ones who uphold the "duty to lie." The Russians, also bypassed by the Renaissance and the Reformation of Europe and progressing rapidly into the twentieth century, have not only enshrined the lie as an official instrument of policy but have taken to rewriting history—of themselves and of other peoples. It was, perhaps, therefore natural that the revolutionary Arab states should have found an affinity with the Soviet Union. To them modern Russia has thrown out its own past and is at loggerheads with the Western world—and is therefore a natural ally of the Arab world.*

* Communism is no obstacle to Arab political philosophy. "Islam is not opposed to Communism from a doctrinal view," writes Dr. Hiram Sharabi, himself an Arab and a professor of Arab Area Studies at Georgetown University in Washington, D.C. "Actually, Islam is peculiarly supple in matters of interpretation and would find no basic conflicts in Communist doctrine save for atheism." Another Arab professor, Nabih Amin Faris, chairman of the Arab Studies Program at the American University of Beirut, wrote: "Many parallels exist between Islam and Communism, and these make a transition from Islam to Communism possible and

It was a combination of the philosophy of the Holy War against the non-Moslem and the "duty to lie for a good result" that led to the formation of terrorist groups to act against Israel. In the Western news media, Arab leaders and spokesmen have managed to build up an image of these groups as "underground fighters."

The Arabs' very signatures to the armistice agreements of 1948 were part of the "lie for a good result." Each of those agreements, according to the preambles of each, was to be a step from war to peace. Each agreement forbade the crossing of the borders, by either the military or paramilitary forces or civilians of either party. Within months, however, Arab infiltrators were beginning to cross into Israel from the Egyptian-held Gaza Strip or Jordan. Perhaps these were the "two thousand spies" Nasser had mentioned to me in our conversation, but their acts were explained away as those of "simple refugees" who were merely returning to their "ancestral orange groves." If any Western journalist

---

even natural, once the individual Moslem shifts his emphasis from the spiritual sphere to the temporal."

Charles Malik, a Lebanese scholar and diplomat who has served as president of the United Nations General Assembly and later taught at Harvard University—a man I have met and admired—is regarded generally as one of the foremost Arab thinkers. He has said: "I don't believe at all that Islam is a bulwark against Communism, any more than Greek Orthodoxy was in Russia. I think that, especially in countries like the Middle East, where you have a number of other factors on which Communism can play—the religious factor is incompetent by itself to withstand the Communist onslaught."

Habib Bourguiba, President of Tunisia, says: "Communism has made a successful compromise with Islam in the Soviet republics of the Caucasus and Central Asia. The Arab masses can be tempted by the apparent general system which simultaneously promises them freedom from European domination, social equality, and better economic conditions, while also appealing to their old instinct for communal living."

or missionary taken in by this propaganda were to have added up the acreage of the groves thus referred to, or the number of houses claimed to have been owned by these infiltrators, he would find that the total exceeded the entire area of Israel or the total number of buildings there.

XIV

I
MEET
THE
TERRORISTS

I was personally exposed to a sample of these Arab grandiose claims in 1960 when I was in Jordan on a United Nations mission to investigate the Arab refugee camps. Driven down the steep, winding hills from Amman to the Arab border of Jerusalem by former Palestinians, I was taken to a tall building behind the barbed wires separating the two countries from which we could look down upon that part of Jerusalem inside Israel. It was a weird experience, like seeing the Jerusalem I knew so well from the other end of a telescope. Here below me was bustling traffic circling around the King David Hotel and the YMCA building. As we looked down upon the busy city, as though from another planet, the Arabs each in turn pointed to a building and said to me, "You see that one? It belongs to me; it was once mine." Having heard this and similar claims from numerous Arabs as to their properties in what was formerly

Palestine during my visits in Jordan, Syria, and Lebanon, I could not resist the temptation to remark wryly, "It seems that every Palestinian who left in 1948 must have been a millionaire."

The plague of terrorism was at first regarded by Israel as a hangover from the 1948 War of Independence, but it soon became apparent that it was in reality part of a calculated Arab policy. Appeals to the United Nations and the Mixed Armistice Commission went unheeded; Israel began to retaliate against the bases from which the terrorists operated.

Terrorism and the terrorist organizations became official in 1955, the year that produced the first Egyptian-Soviet arms deal. The bases of the Fedayeen ("Sacrificers") were located in the Gaza Strip under the command of Major Mustafa Mohammed Bafiz, chief of Egyptian intelligence in that area. A large proportion of its members were murderers and criminals specially released from prison on condition that they undertook terrorist operations inside Israel. Within a short time other Fedayeen bases were organized in Jordan, Syria, and Lebanon, but all were under Egyptian control. In Jordan, they were the direct responsibility of Major Salah Mustafa, the Egyptian military attaché there. On August 31, 1955, Cairo Radio officially revealed to the Egyptians and to the world the new military tactic:

> Egypt has decided to dispatch her heroes, the disciples of Pharaoh and the sons of Islam, and they will cleanse the land of Palestine. Therefore ready yourselves; shed tears, cry out and weep, O Israel, because your day of liquidation is near. Thus we have decided and thus is our belief. . . . The Egyptian

Fedayeen have begun their activities inside the territory of Israel after repeated clashes on the border during the past week. The Egyptian Fedayeen have penetrated into Jewish settlements spread out in the Negev. . . . The Egyptian Fedayeen sowed fear and consternation among the citizens of Israel.

It was the beginning of official Arab exaggeration, which was to mislead the Arab population and cause them to underestimate Israel. Two days later Cairo Radio again boasted: "The forces of the Egyptian Fedayeen moved towards Israel, reached Tel Aviv, and caused heavy casualties to Israel along the border between Gaza and Tel Aviv."

The United Nations Chief of Staff, General E. L. M. Burns, quickly realized the dangers inherent in this official sponsorship of terrorism. He informed Israel on April 8, 1956, that he had protested to the Egyptian government, adding that "I consider that if Egypt ordered these Fedayeen raids, she has now put herself in the position of an aggressor."

Nasser's reply followed six weeks later, on May 28, when he declared: "The Fedayeen, the Palestine army, which started as a small force of a thousand men last year, is today great in numbers and training equipment. I believe in the strength, the ability, the loyalty, and the courage of this army. Its soldiers will be responsible for taking revenge for their homeland and people." A few weeks later he again referred to the Fedayeen, but this time revealed the wider use to which Arab nationalist and revolutionary terrorism would be put: "We are obliged to be strong in order to liberate the entire Arab land from Morocco to Baghdad" (BBC Radio Monitoring Service).

These and similar official pronouncements were being

aired over the official Cairo Radio at the very hour I was meeting with Nasser in his home outside of Cairo, when he bluntly accused the Israelis of inciting the border action in Gaza.

"I had to transfer money for the building program of schools to the Gaza front for arms to protect my people" (the Palestine refugees), Nasser complained to me. My personal observations from visiting in Gaza, in fact, revealed the desolation resulting from the cold indifference of the Egyptian government to the condition of the refugees, who were not permitted to leave the area, even to visit Egypt.

It was the murderous activities of the Fedayeen which led directly to the Sinai war of 1956, but Egypt's defeat did not mean the end of the organization of Arab terrorism against Israel. With the second rearming of Egypt by the Soviet Union, sabotage and terrorist units made up largely of Palestinian refugees were established in Egypt, Syria, Iraq, and other Arab countries. They were trained by Egyptian officers and equipped with Soviet weapons. In 1956 Nasser urged the Arab League to establish the Palestine Liberation Organization, a political group, and its military arm, the Palestine Liberation Army.

In 1960 I was appointed consultant at the United Nations headquarters in New York to Dr. John H. Davis, director of UNRWA. At the Gotham Bank in New York, where I was chairman, I found one of the members of the board was an executive of an oil company with large Middle East holdings. After he had complained to me that his company's operations were penalized by the lack of men who could do physical labor in the oil fields, I suggested that manual labor was available in the refugee camps, after some elementary training. Under the leadership of David Shepard, then a vice-president of Standard Oil Company, and Thomas Barger, former president of ARAMCO (American Arabian Oil Company), a group of major oil companies operating in the Middle East agreed to contribute funds to UNRWA to establish vocational training schools to prepare refugees in the Jordanian camps for work in the oil fields of Kuwait and Saudi Arabia. The program managed to move some thousands of refugees out of the camps into employment by oil companies. But unfortunately, my plan to have them removed from the UNRWA rolls backfired, as their families who remained behind in the camps kept their ration cards and continued to draw assistance from UNRWA. Only after Israel occupied the areas containing the camps was it learned that the Arab refugee workers in Saudi Arabia and Kuwait sent their substantial salaries back to their families, who nevertheless continued to draw UNRWA rations.

The terrorist leaders and the Arab governments make no secret of the fact that they are using many of the camps, when strategically located, as military training centers to prepare for assaults on Israel. The terrorists operate freely in the southeastern and southwestern regions of Lebanon and in the refugee camps scattered throughout the country, where the commando organizations not only recruit and train but also run the camps and in effect control the surrounding Lebanese territory. These refugee camps and villages, in effect, have become extraterritorial enclaves as far as Lebanese sovereignty is concerned. Photos have been released and have appeared in *The New York Times* and other publications and on TV, showing terrorists training in refugee camps with youths using automatic weapons, explosives, and guerrilla tactics. One was at the Ain Hilweh Palestine refugee camp near Sidon in Lebanon, which I had visited. No effort has been made by the Lebanon government or by the guerrilla leaders to hide the fact that fifteen refugee camps in Lebanon are now in control of the military.

While in Beirut completing my report for the Department of State in the American embassy, I ran into members of the guerrillas openly selling propaganda pamphlets on the streets. Even at the sumptuous hotels, the St. George and the Phoenicia, the pamphlets were on sale in the lobbies; they contained vivid, detailed, illustrated instructions on how to kill Israelis. One of the photographs in the training manual showed a picture of the explosion of an Israeli bus which killed sixteen children and a doctor. The caption underneath the picture read: "A successful operation."

The pre-emption of these UNRWA camps as terrorist training centers is done under the noses of the UNRWA operators, who are responsible for the camps and the refugees. The irony of this is that the camps are supported by an arm of the United Nations, the world's international peace organization. Seventy percent of the funds are supplied by the taxpayers of the United States, which means that American citizens are defraying most of the cost for camps openly and avowedly used to prepare and incite war against a neighbor country and a fellow United Nations member. Little or no objection has been raised by the UNRWA directors, who are, from my proved observation, working hand in hand with the Arab governments and terrorist leaders. Here is final proof of the breakdown and obsolescence of UNRWA, a dated international body whose phasing out is long overdue.

While the Fedayeen and the Palestine Liberation organization were sponsored, trained, and equipped by Egypt, the Syrians set about more quietly organizing their own guerrilla organization—the Fatah—which had been organized by Yasir Arafat among fellow Palestine Arab students in Germany and Austria in 1955. The word "Fatah" means "conquest" but is also the reverse initials of the Palestine Liberation Movement in Arabic. It was at first a small, extremely radical political group, but by the beginning of 1965 it received the semiofficial sponsorship of Syrian intelligence, which set about helping Arafat establish a military arm—the Asifa storm troopers. With the establishment of a new radical government in Damascus in 1966, the sponsorship became official. Unlike other groups which did more talking than acting, Fatah became more active against Israel and also more vocally critical of the other Arab governments. Yet other terrorist groups came into being in the years following 1966, the best known of them being the left-wing Popular Front for the Liberation of Palestine, whose members have concentrated on attacks against and the hijacking of aircraft and on violent acts against Israeli civilians, such as the deliberate ambush of a school bus and the murder of eight schoolchildren and four teachers.

While Arafat saw these violent acts abroad as harmful public relations, the Popular Front moved ever further to the left. Its leader, Dr. George Habash, admitted in interviews with Western journalists that his movement regarded its enemy not only to be "Israel and Zionism" but also imperialism, under which he includes the United States and Great Britain, the Soviet Union and Hussein. His aim, he admitted, is to turn the Middle East into another Vietnam, even if this involves the risk of a third world war.

While the brand of Communism taught to Fatah members is the gospel from Moscow, Dr. Habash's followers are said to look to Peking for their inspiration. In September 1970, this took the form of hijacking and blowing up two passenger planes of the BOAC and one each of Swissair and TWA. An Israel El Al hijacking was thwarted by the instant shooting of the hijacker and the capture of his female companion. The 550 passengers—men, women and children—were citizens of England, Switzerland, the United States, and Israel. They were kept captive by the terrorists under primitive conditions in their planes in a boiling sun for five days outside Amman.

All but 56 were then taken to Amman and hidden in a refugee camp, helpless victims caught in the center of Jordan's bloody civil war. The defeat of the commandos by King Hussein's army made their eventual rescue possible, but only after exchange of prisoners and payment of secret blackmail money.

XV

RUSSIA
BACKS
THE
TERRORISTS

For the Russians, the terrorist organizations and their un-controlled activities have become an increasing source of worry, and the Kremlin has managed to straddle in its attitude toward them. The Soviet Union has had considerable experience with guerrilla organizations. During World War II, the partisans, under Russian control, did valiant work behind the Nazi lines, attacking German soldiers, military installations, and communications networks. Political control, however, always remained firmly in Russian hands. The Russians had reason enough to be wary of guerrilla leaders who do not accept Russian political control. One partisan leader who "got away" and took his own independent political line was Tito of Yugoslavia.

In 1949 Tito broke out from under the yoke of Stalin and has continued to maintain his independence ever since. To determine whether the Stalin-Tito break was a fraud or a real break, I was sent that year to Yugoslavia by the Department of State. My report, which recommended that we "assist in pushing the Iron Curtain back to the Dalmatian Coast," was instrumental in our government's decision to support the plucky Communist leader who had first won his stripes by standing up to Hitler's hordes. My meetings with Tito and his valiant young partisans were my first experience in seeing a young, courageous small nation hold its ground against a monolithic "partner."

During the ten years between the Sinai campaign and the Six-Day War, the Arabs used the Fedayeen for both terror and intelligence against Israel. The Soviet Union, however, opposed the activities of the Fedayeen, fearing the inevitable Israeli retaliation against Nasser's Egypt.

After the war, however, the attitude of Moscow toward the terrorists began to change slowly, though apparently with some misgivings and soul-searching in the Kremlin. For these were "guerrilla" movements without Russian political commissars attached to them, even though they were armed with Soviet weapons. Furthermore, at a time when the Soviet Union was pressing for a "political solution" to the Middle East problem, Arafat was shouting loudly for the liquidation of Israel, while Dr. George Habash, leader of the Popular Front for the Liberation of Palestine, a Peking-inspired Marxist, was even speaking critically of Nasser, Moscow's ally.

As the months passed, however, the strategists in the Kremlin became aware of several new developments. The terrorist organizations, till then equipped with Russian-made weapons via Egypt and Syria, threatened to accept arms from China if not supplied directly from Russia.

Some members of the Popular Front were even sent to Peking for training in guerrilla tactics. The Israelis began discovering Chinese weapons and Chinese food on the bodies of terrorists killed while trying to cross into Israeli-held territory. Another factor was the growing popularity of Arafat and his Fatah. Whereas some years previously the name most often heard on Arab lips was that of Nasser, the more fashionable name now was Arafat.

A temporary cooling off of Russian enthusiasm for Fatah was apparent in the early part of 1969 when, instead of the tactic of merely training the guerrillas, Syria began encouraging terrorists to cross the Syrian-Israeli cease-fire lines instead of via Jordan and Lebanon. This was too much like the situation prior to the Six-Day War.

Arafat's prestige, however, continued to grow, and the Arab world was all too ready to believe his gross exaggerations of the results achieved by his men; it believed that he and his Fatah were the only Arabs getting action against the Israelis and that the Russians were only talking—and about a political solution at that. If the Fatah was so successful, according to its own statements, Arafat would be the Arab saviour, the modern Saladin.

In December 1969 Nasser dramatically stalked out of a meeting of the heads of Arab nations in Rabat, Morocco, which was convened for the purpose of supporting his military program to attack and destroy the common enemy, Israel. The king of Saudi Arabia and the ruler of Kuwait, when faced by Nasser with a "demand" for $360,000,000 to implement his military equipment for the assault, refused point-blank. Arab unity in opposition to Israel is one thing; support by the oil-rich rulers of Nasser's phony socialism to take over the power of the Arab world is quite another.

The drama surrounding Nasser's abrupt walkout of the Rabat meeting was nothing, however, compared to the pomp and power play put on by Arafat in his entrance to the conclave. Dressed in colorful leopard-spot camouflage uniform and "keffiyah" headdress of the Jordanian fighters, this five-foot-four leader, sporting a five-day growth of beard, arrived with gun on shoulder, flanked by two bodyguards. Arafat stole the show. Nasser smirked and departed. Arafat's bravado and decor to the contrary notwithstanding, he had won only "love and sympathy" from the oil moguls according to his complaint; Libya alone offered his terrorist gangs a ten-million-dollar pledge. But the terrorist bandwagon was too impressive for the Soviets not to climb aboard. Slowly Soviet support swung back in favor of Arafat's guerrillas. In the early months of 1970, the Kremlin backed the terrorists in their efforts to gain bases in Lebanon and weaken Hussein in Jordan.

During the savage civil war between the guerrillas and King Hussein's Bedouin troops in Jordan in September 1970, Moscow was careful not to take sides but to confine its pronouncements to a warning directed to the United States not to intervene in Jordan, adding pious hopes that the war flames would die down. But the White House finally awoke to the danger of the terrorists' capture and explosion of its prodigious interests in the Middle East and sped the Sixth Fleet of fifty ships and 2000 men to the Mediterranean coast. It also alerted American airborne troops in Turkey and Germany. President Nixon personally injected himself into the impending crisis by visiting the Middle East. In his speech to the sailors on the *Saratoga* on September 29, the President said, "The fact that we were successful is the fact that you were there." The "there" meant in the

Mediterranean ready to spring to King Hussein's defense, whose forces knocked out from sixty to ninety of the Syrian tanks that had rolled into Jordan.

The Russians got the message. The Syrians were pressured to withdraw their forces from Jordan. Iraq, which had an army of 12,000 inside Jordan, was prevailed upon to immobilize it. The United States also secretly managed to get word to the Israelis that it "did not discourage" the massing of their armor on the northern Jordan frontiers and flying missions over the Syrian invasion forces.

What was left of the ninety-day truce was torpedoed by the terrorists. The civil war in Jordan further deflated Hussein's power and President Nasser, stricken at the airport as he was bidding the Arab leaders and Arafat adieu, died on September 28, having engineered an accord between them. It was the flamboyant Arab leader's last official act.

The terms of the accord constituted a significant victory for the embattled Palestinian guerrillas, for it ironically assured them of the concerted support of the Arab world until "full liberation and victory over the aggressive Israeli army." The upshot of the civil war, aside from the paroxysm of slaughter, was to coalesce the terrorists' program with the Arab leaders to turn their aggression against the common enemy, Israel. Item No. 14 in the text of the agreement signed in Cairo on September 28 by nine Arab countries and Yasir Arafat, head of the Palestinian guerrillas, reads, "The goal is the consolidation of the Palestine revolution, backing it until it achieves its objectives of full liberation and the defeat of the aggressive Israeli enemy."

If the civil war in Jordan in 1970 blew the Russians' timetable in the Middle East sky-high, they have no one to blame but themselves. The repeated rejection by the guerrilla leaders of the king's offers of compromise must have had the backing of the Kremlin, which was primarily responsible for the blood bath. The Russians encouraged the guerrilla leaders to push King Hussein to the brink, where he had a choice of either abdicating his leadership to them or unleashing his Bedouin troops against the commandos. The result was fire and slaughter, which indiscriminately hit the Jordanian population, refugees in the camps, as well as the terrorists.

The firebrand guerrillas took a beating, but the setback may be only temporary. Hussein's skin and throne were saved by a combination of his army and the timely threat of intervention by outside forces, Israel and the United States.

But the most crucial and significant lesson that emerged from the civil war in Jordan was the sudden tightening and resolution of U.S. policy in the Middle East, when we informed the Kremlin in stern language that they would face serious consequences if they did not pull back their clients, Syria and Iraq, from the conflict. The United States also indicated in concrete terms its appreciation of Israel's value as a friend in the area when it showed its satisfaction when Israel began massing its army on the northern Jordan border. That the Kremlin backed away in the face of this new U.S. posture and firmness can hardly be lost on the policy makers in Washington.

XVI

MEDITERRANEAN—
BOILING
WATERS

To break out of its deep freeze into warm-water ports has been a two-century-old obsession of the Russian leaders. For with thousands of miles of sea coasts, this giant state is nevertheless completely blocked from entry to the world's oceans and sea lanes. The Baltic Sea is blocked by the Danish straits. The Barent Sea in the north with its winter ice is a long and hard way round to the Atlantic Ocean even in the short summer months. This, too, can be blockaded in the narrow area between Scotland, Iceland, and Greenland. In the Far East, ships on the way out from Russia to the Pacific are hemmed in by a chain of Japanese islands.

The Black Sea, where almost all of Russia's year-round ice-free ports are to be found, is locked in by the Bosporus and the Dardanelles, but this has not today blocked Russia's long-range strategic aims.

The view of the Mediterranean from Moscow is of a far-reaching enclave in the heart of the Eurasian land mass. From it, American aircraft carriers can reach the centers of Russia, as well as southern Europe and the Balkans, target areas close to the nerve centers of the Soviet. In the 1950's before the intercontinental missiles crystalized the "Balance of Terror," the American Sixth Fleet was a prime atomic threat to the USSR. That was before the Soviets had begun to throw their naval weight around in the Mediterranean, when Russia's "naval presence" was confined to seemingly innocent fishing vessels (the Soviet Union has the world's largest fishing fleet) but with their hulls crammed with electronic gear to keep an eye on United States and NATO ship movements. Then comes a small submarine fleet, the vessels being sneaked in through the Straits of Gibraltar and based in a secret cove in Albania. When that country turned away from Moscow and threw in its lot with Peking, alternate friendly ports had to be found.

Nasser's well-timed offer in 1954 of Alexandria and Port Said was gladly accepted, and from that moment on the Soviet naval presence in the Middle East grew rapidly. Since those early days a decade and a half ago, the Russian Mediterranean fleet has grown in numbers and firepower. Its presence has been accompanied by thundering demands that the U.S. Sixth Fleet evacuate the Mediterranean, accompanied by a propaganda obbligato that the "Russian fleet is the most modern today and is able to fulfill any task at sea."

While the possibility of a clash between the Soviet Navy and the Sixth Fleet today seems remote, should it arise the Soviet fleet would find itself enclosed in a trap, cut off from all of its sources of supplies and reinforcements. On the other hand, the U.S. would have no difficulty in reinforcing its supplies at will from the Atlantic Ocean without impinging on its obligations in other seas. To this must be added the fleets of NATO countries in the Mediterranean which constitute a major threat to Soviet intentions.

While on a government mission in Lebanon in 1958, I saw firsthand the decisive power of the American Sixth Fleet. The unhesitating step then taken by Eisenhower and Dulles in unloading the American marines on the shores of Beirut produced the exact effect intended. And this without the Arabs, or the vaunted United States sharpshooters, firing a single shot. The very presence of the Sixth Fleet and the landing in force of the green-uniformed marines were enough to force Nasser's agents to rapidly abandon his intended grab of Lebanon. The threat alone was enough to obviate military action and also to convince every other Arab leader, at least before the Russian squadron complicated the issue, that the Sixth Fleet was no empty naval gesture parading along the Mediterranean; that the United States was ready to back up its power with performance; and that it was not in any sense prepared to relinquish its strong presence in the Middle East by default to the Russians or to anyone else.

The decisive results from this positive United States stance should have served as a blueprint to be applied in an area that is crying out for American firmness. Since then, the Russian Navy has through maneuvering and propaganda succeeded in conveying the impression that the powerful United States Sixth Fleet is on the defensive. Besides boosting the morale of the Kremlin's protégés in Syria, Algiers, Iraq, and Egypt, it has also served to frighten some military observers into accepting the fallacy that the Russian Navy is prepared to operate at will from Gibraltar all the way to the Persian Gulf, while the Sixth Fleet will sit as an idle spectator.

The Greek poets described its waters as "wine-dark," while the Romans called it *Mare Nostrum*—Our Sea. To the ancient Hebrews and in classical Arabic it was the Great Sea. To most of the world it is known as the Middle Sea or the Middle Land Sea, for that is the meaning of the Mediterranean, the largest of the inland seas, which has always been a fulcrum in the struggle between the great powers of the era. Its importance has never diminished, from the days of land power, through sea power and air power, to today's age of the missile.

The Soviet Union is now intent on making it into "their sea." With the Kremlin firmly rooted in Egypt, Syria, and Algeria, as well as in Yemen on the Red Sea and Iraq with its outlet on the Persian Gulf, the movement of the Red Fleet in the waters as an open adversary constitutes a growing threat to the Western world that cannot be disregarded. Soviet aims in these waters are not only to strengthen their Arab clients but also to further their own strategic aims southward.

The Mediterranean has been a highway for commerce as early as four thousand years ago, when the Phoenicians crisscrossed its tideless water, plying their trade with their city colonies dotted along its shores. They even sailed bravely past its western portals into the Atlantic Ocean.

For the Greeks and Romans also, the Mediterranean was used for transport of goods and soldiers, but it was more a quiet lake than a throughway. Some centuries later, it became a corridor again to carry the commerce of the Orient over its peaceful waters to Europe. With the opening up of the direct sea route around the Cape of Good Hope in the late fifteenth century, the Mediterranean again lost its importance as a communications link for European trade, but once again won it back in 1869, with the opening of the Suez Canal.

For Great Britain the Mediterranean was a vital staging post on the road to its eastern empire, and even today, Great Britain is fighting hard to maintain its hold on Gibraltar, guarding the western approaches to the Mediterranean.

United States interest in the Mediterranean began in the very first days of the nation's existence. Thomas Jefferson, while a member of George Washington's cabinet, objected strongly to the United States continuing to pay ransom and tribute to the Barbary pirates of Algiers, Tripoli and Morocco. Captain William Bainbridge had even been forced to carry Algerine tribute to Constantinople in the frigate *George Washington,* and to fly the Ottoman flag while doing so. As President, Jefferson stiffened American policy and sent young Stephen Decatur to Tripoli in 1801. Bainbridge's frigate, the *Philadelphia,* had run aground, and the commander and his fleet were imprisoned in Tripoli. Decatur and his party boarded the ship and set it afire to prevent its use by the pirates. William Easton, a former U.S. consul in Tunis, led a small land force from Egypt to attack the Barbary pirates from the rear. After a grueling march through the desert, he got as far as Derna before the humiliating peace of 1805 was concluded. The Algerine War was resumed in 1815, and Decatur again played a leading role. The ruler of Algeria finally agreed to end tribute and ransom demands from the United States.

American vital interests in the Middle East were quickened in the twentieth century. In both World War I and World War II, the Mediterranean and the Middle East were important theaters of fighting. In the early days of this century the Germans had sought to expand their influence via the Berlin-to-Baghdad railway. In 1917, they and their Turkish allies were stopped by General Allenby's campaign in Palestine. The turning point of World War II was not at Stalingrad, the scene of the heroic Russian stand against the Nazis, but at El Alamein, in the western desert of Egypt, where British guns and American tanks diverted from other hard-pressed battlegrounds in the European theater of war turned the tide of Field Marshal Rommel's advance.

Immediately following World War II, United States interest was concentrated in Turkey and Greece, where the Marshall Plan and the Truman Doctrine were introduced to strengthen NATO allies against Communist penetration. America's expanding oil interest in Saudi Arabia then seemed safe from Soviet manipulation. This European defense posture resulted in the establishment of the U.S. Sixth Fleet in the Mediterranean, to guard what Churchill described during the war as the "soft underbelly of Europe." The Sixth Fleet both strengthens the western sector of that underbelly and stands as a potential threat to the "soft underbelly" of Eastern Europe. The Sixth has become a watchword, underscoring the Mediterranean as a continuing focal point of American interest. And now, the U.S. Seventh Fleet is to be moved from the Far East to the Indian Ocean and the Persian Gulf, at the end of the southern exit from this vital sea.

Russian interest in the Mediterranean has always been a

key to the extension of Russian policy southward, in the Black Sea and the Dardanelles. When Turkey declared war on Russia in 1768, the Empress Catherine II ordered a fleet sent from the Baltic around the whole of Europe to the eastern Mediterranean, to back up her land armies moving to the Danube. The activities of both land and sea forces in the area were crowned with success, but while the fleet occupied strategic places in the Aegean archipelago and destroyed the Turkish fleet, it did not succeed in forcing the Dardanelles to join up with the Russian land troops.

Catherine II's successor, Czar Paul, reversed her policy: instead of warring with the Turks, he allied Russia with Turkey in support of England's war against Napoleon. Under a special convention for joint action with the Ottoman Empire, the Turks agreed to permit the Russian fleet to sail through the Bosporus and the Dardanelles, at the same time undertaking to keep the straits closed to the warships of other nations. The Russian Black Sea squadron, accompanied by Turkish vessels, sailed into the Adriatic arm of the Mediterranean in 1798 and drove the French from the Ionian Islands, where Admiral Feodor Ushakov established a republic, formally under Turkish but in actual fact under Russian control. It was the first instance of direct Russian interest in a Mediterranean land—but not the last. The following year a Russian naval base was set up in the Adriatic. This step accomplished, Paul looked further afield in the Mediterranean: he became patron of the Order of the Knights of Saint John—the Maltese Knights—who owned the island of Malta. But Great Britain took control of both Malta and the Ionian Islands at the end of the Napoleonic wars.

Russia's advances were further blocked as a result of the

Crimean war, a campaign outstanding for the military incompetence of the generals on both sides. Under the Treaty of Paris (1856), which ended that war, Russia lost the right to maintain a fleet in the Black Sea, which was neutralized. Both the Bosporus and Dardanelles were now closed to warships of all nations, including Russia.

To reverse the effects of an edict forbidding Russian warships to use the narrow Turkish straits, Czar Alexander III instructed his ambassador to sign the Constantinople Convention of 1888 laying down the ground rules for passage through the Suez Canal, the first article of which reads: "The Suez Maritime Canal shall always be free and open, in time of war as in time of peace, to every vessel of commerce or of war, without distinction of flag. The Canal shall never be subject to the exercise of the right of blockade."

In the heyday of the British Empire it was said that "Trade follows the flag"—the flag being aboard the warships. Russia's recent re-entry into the Mediterranean reversed this process. First came the "trade," the Soviet guns for Egyptian cotton which quickly developed into a veritable flood of Soviet armaments to Egypt. Then came the "flag," the appearance at Egyptian ports of Russian naval vessels, at first on "courtesy" and "good-will" calls, but later on almost permanent visits. It was this constant movement of ships and crews in and out of Port Said delivering armaments to Egypt which influenced Israel to halt her retaliatory bombing along the eastern bank of the Suez Canal short of Port Said. The aim was, of course, to avoid "incidents" with the Russians.

The Mediterranean squadron of the Russian fleet has also used Port Said and Alexandria as useful way stations on their watch patrols over the activities of the American Sixth Fleet. The Russian ships were later joined on this surveillance task by Russian pilots flying Russian-built aircraft marked with Egyptian air-force insignia from air bases within Egypt. This was escalated to the active use of Soviet pilots flying operational flights within Egypt, posing a serious threat to Israel and enhancing the danger of a Soviet-Israeli clash.

American naval policy makers have recently expressed their concern over Russia's progress in the Mediterranean as part of their program to encircle Western defensive and economic positions.*

While the mainstay of the American Sixth Fleet in the Mediterranean and of the fleets elsewhere is the aircraft carrier, the Soviet Union was slow to develop this type of naval vessel. Instead, they have developed another type of war vessel—the 20,000-ton helicopter carrier. Russia's carriers, the *Moskva* and the *Leningrad,* which have been cruising

---

* In a speech in New York in January 1968, Admiral John S. M. McCain, Jr., commander in chief of U.S. naval forces in Europe, stated that Soviet naval activities in the Mediterranean were not a direct result of the Israel–Arab war but rather of long-range Soviet strategic planning and ambition. They also gave the Arabs a feeling that they were getting firm support. In a report to Congress before leaving his post, former Secretary of Defense Robert S. McNamara called the Soviet navy buildup in the Mediterranean "a diplomatic gesture aimed at recouping political losses suffered as a result of Moscow's inability to forestall Israel's victory." He warned that "the Soviet Union's partisan political position on Middle Eastern questions, its increased naval presence in the Mediterranean, its intervention in the conflict in Yemen and its efforts to reduce or supplant Western influence generally, have contributed to instability in the region."

U.S. Rear Admiral Allen F. Fleming, discussing the large number of Soviet submarines always in the Mediterranean, which it is the task of his air surveillance units to watch, states that "their threat is more political than military. They are trying to extend their influence through the deployment of naval forces. A fleet is a good way of extending spheres of influence. Historically, this has always been a part of sea power."

the Mediterranean, could quickly put ashore large numbers of Soviet troops if these were required to back up Moscow's policies.

The helicopter carriers are, however, primarily designed for antisubmarine warfare, to be used as a defense against missile-carrying submarines such as those equipped with Polaris missiles. They are therefore in the Mediterranean as part of Russia's anti-Western strategy, in which the Mideast conflict is used for tactical reasons.

The normal complement of the Soviet squadron is at least one cruiser of the 25,000-ton *Sverdlov* class and about ten escorts of which three or four have surface-to-surface or surface-to-air missiles. There are also about ten submarines, one or two of which might be nuclear-powered.

The effectiveness of the surface-to-surface missiles aboard Russian warships was illustrated by the sinking of the Israeli destroyer *Elath* in October 1967 by Soviet-made Styx missiles fired from a Soviet-built Egyptian torpedo boat.

To keep a close eye on the movements of Soviet warships in the Mediterranean, which themselves keep a close eye on the United States and NATO warships, NATO in 1968 set up COMFAIRMED—Commander Fleet Air Mediterranean—which flies Neptune and Orion aircraft equipped with electronic detection equipment, in constant watch.

The Communist party newspaper *Pravda* in a lengthy article published in November 1968 wrote that the Soviet Navy was in the Mediterranean to safeguard Russian interests in the region and was there "with the approval and in accordance with the interests of the Arab States.*

* "Soviet ships entered the sea on the strength of the USSR's sovereign right to make use of this open sea. We have a full right to this from

The Russian Mediterranean squadron has already achieved part of its purpose in neutralizing the Sixth Fleet. The United States could not today with impunity repeat a landing of marines in Beirut as it did in 1958, when Lebanon felt endangered by Nasser-sponsored terrorists.

Nine years later when both the American Sixth and Russian fleets were close together in the eastern Mediterranean at the time of the Six-Day War, President Johnson used the Washington-Moscow "hot line" to obviate a clash between the two supernavies. In 1969, when Lebanon's integrity was again threatened by Syria-based guerrillas, the presence of the Russian warships, in increased strength and numbers, immobilized any possible American aid even if asked for.

The simultaneous presence of vessels from the Sixth Fleet and from other members of the NATO Western alliance, confronting the Soviet squadron in the waters of the Mediterranean (each for its own national purposes quite separate from the Arab-Israel conflict), has already led to "accidents" between them which threaten increasingly to boil over into diplomatic "incidents." Soviet aircraft based on Egyptian airfields have frequently buzzed American aircraft carriers while United States planes take off or land. A growing number of near-misses and near air-collisions are being noted in the fleet logs. Russian vessels have sailed perilously close to Western ships on maneuvers requiring skillful last-minute diversions to escape tragedy. Soviet submarines have sur-

---

the historical, political, economic, and geographical points of view. As a Black Sea and, in this sense, a Mediterranean power, it is closely connected with all problems involving the interests of the peoples of this area of Europe, Africa, and Asia." The Soviet Union, the paper said, "is directly interested in insuring the security of its southern borders."

faced in the midst of maneuvering NATO ships, and in at least one instance a collision has been reported. At the beginning of 1970 a Soviet submarine was reported afloat in the western Mediterranean with its bow shorn off, surrounded by a screen of Russian vessels. What was not reported at the time was that the accident occurred when the Russian sub surfaced suddenly in front of an oncoming NATO vessel—Russian brinkmanship or Russian roulette?

The Soviet Union is not content to sit back and wait for Western withdrawal from the Mediterranean and the Middle East. The British have departed, or are departing; the French were forced out of Algeria. The Americans, however, remain in the Mediterranean and in the Saudi Arabia oil fields, and, in the view from Moscow, are still to be ousted. Through their Arab allies, the Russians are undermining pro-Western Arab governments. The latest successful example was the Libyan revolt in early 1970, an anti-Western move having nothing at all to do with the Arab-Israel conflict.

Another major sector of the Mediterranean front was lost to the West when the revolt of the Libyan army officers ousted the pro-Western king at the beginning of 1970. The script could not have been written better in Moscow. The inexperienced Libyan army leaders immediately called for the assistance of their Egyptian brother officers to help them with "advisors," who themselves are backed up by Soviet advisors. Their first step was to demand the immediate withdrawal of the Americans from the Wheelus U.S. Air Force base, not far from the important port of Tripoli. Wheelus, one of the largest air bases in the world, had been of overriding importance in the U.S. Air Force training program.

The French were quick to see the Wheelus vacuum as an

economic and political opportunity (since they had been foiled some months earlier in an attempt to barter oil concessions in Iraq for Mirage aircraft). Franco-Libyan negotiations were immediately opened, with the Libyan team reportedly headed by Egyptian intelligence agents. Moscow was content to allow Paris to move in, recognizing Gaullist and post-Gaullist France as the least dangerous to itself in the East-West political lineup.

From a sea-level view, the Libyan revolt represents a danger to the West. The ports of Tripoli and Bengasi will henceforth be barred to ships of the U.S. Sixth Fleet and NATO vessels, while those of the Soviet Mediterranean squadron will be welcomed. The Russian ships will now find friends along almost the entire stretch of the southern Mediterranean coastline, from Port Said in Egypt to Oran in Algeria, new warm-water ports for Soviet domination.

The irony of the situation is that the Soviet Union has made full use of its rights, under international law, to sail its squadron in the Mediterranean and has had the impertinence at the same time to demand withdrawal of the U.S. Sixth fleet from those waters. And yet, American warships have as much right to sail in the Black Sea bordering the Soviet as Russian ships have to sail in the Mediterranean, but we have never really used that right. Only occasionally does a token pair of destroyers sail through the Bosporus into the Black Sea, cruise around timorously for a day or so, and then leave.

If units of the Sixth Fleet were more often to enter and show a more permanent presence in the Black Sea, the Russians could not fail to understand, and it would be a weighty barter point for Soviet-United States discussions. It would also immeasurably strengthen the determination of countries such as Romania to show an added measure of independence from Moscow. Soviet demands for withdrawal of the Sixth Fleet could then be countered by an American offer to withdraw the Sixth Fleet from the Black Sea if the Soviet squadron were to withdraw from the Mediterranean. Both fleets would be entitled to "courtesy" visits but would not serve as permanent politically maneuvering forces.

The Soviets now have a junior partner in the Egyptian navy, equipped and trained by the Russians and protected from Israeli bombing at the present stage by the very presence in Egyptian harbors of the Russian ships and sailors, and now with Soviet pilots flying operational missions over Egypt also. To counter the threat of this Arab fleet, the Israelis were sufficiently determined to strengthen their limited naval forces to take the risk of mounting a James Bond operation, smuggling five gunboats they had purchased from France out of a French port against the wishes of the French authorities in Paris, who were intent on building up their friendship among the Arabs at the expense of Israel.

For the Soviet Union, the Mediterranean has wider uses than merely keeping an eye on the U.S. Sixth Fleet and bolstering the morale and military power of the Arab states. It is also a passageway through which the Russians aim to fill the power vacuum that will be created by the final British withdrawal from the Persian Gulf by 1971. But to carry out this wider strategic aim, the USSR needs the Suez Canal as an open, functioning waterway. With Israeli troops on its eastern bank, the Russians in their fury and frustration seem hell-bent to force its opening, if not by political machinations with the United States, then by blasting it open, the consequences of which could convulse the world.

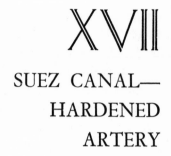

XVII

SUEZ CANAL— HARDENED ARTERY

The Suez Canal was opened in 1869, though not to the strains of *Aida,* which Giuseppe Verdi was commissioned to write for the occasion—*Aida* was not heard until 1871. Today, a century later, the musical strains of the postponed celebration have been replaced by the staccato of machine guns, the thunder of artillery, and the roar of jet warplanes over the waterway.

Besides being the only shipping canal in the world to have had an opera written especially for its opening, the Suez can chalk up to its credit other firsts and world records. It is twice as long as the Panama Canal—100.6 miles as against Panama's 50 miles. It is twice as wide—197 feet as against 110 feet (but it is a couple of feet shallower and has no locks, being sea level all the way).

The present Suez Canal also is the oldest, with a history going back four thousand years.

Until a few years ago, it was Western Europe to whom the Suez Canal was of vital economic and strategic importance. Today it is the Soviet Union, which has most at stake in its rapid reopening. Blocked and closed since June 1967, it is a bottleneck in the path of Russia's strategic goal in southern and southeastern Asia.

The advantages of a canal linking the Mediterranean with the Red Sea were known to the ancient Egyptians almost thirty-four centuries ago. With the slave labor then available, the digging of a giant ditch for the builders of the pyramids was no insuperable problem. At that time the Red Sea penetrated into the present Lake Timsah, and the man-made cut therefore extended from present Port Said to the lake. As the Red Sea waters retreated, the canal was lengthened by Darius I and was repaired several times in subsequent centuries until it was finally abandoned in the eighth century.

The idea of a maritime canal was revived by Ferdinand de Lesseps, who planned and supervised its construction in the decade from 1859 to 1869. The majority of the shares in the Suez Canal Maritime Canal Company was purchased for Great Britain by Prime Minister Disraeli, who realized its importance for the British Empire as the most important link between London and India, the newly acquired "brightest jewel in the British Imperial Crown."

The opening of the canal transformed the Mediterranean from a gigantic lake that was important only to its littoral states into a channel that linked Europe with the Orient. Although only wide enough for one-way passage, the waterway was quickly used alternately for traffic bound both east and west, taking personnel and industrial goods to the East and bringing back raw materials to keep the wheels of European industry turning. For the naval forces of the European countries, and especially for the British Navy, Suez was a vital link. Without this passageway, European industry would not have developed as rapidly as it did; the colonies exploited by the European empires in eastern Africa and Asia would have slept on for years more.

During World War I and World War II, the Suez was an invaluable channel in the Allies' fight against Germany. Because the northern port of Murmansk was icebound much of the year, the Suez became a vital passageway for the transportation of American lend-lease supplies to the Soviet Union pumped into Russia through the warm-water ports of Iran. During World War I Germany and its Turkish ally reached for the waterway in a major but aborted operation via Palestine. In World War II, Hitler's armies tried to wrest it from the Allies in a major drive through Italy, North Africa, and the Western Desert of Egypt, coming within a few miles of the Suez in 1944.

My work in the American embassy in Ankara took me frequently to Cairo, and I was there at the famed Shepheard's Hotel when Field Marshal Rommel and his Nazi forces reached El Alamein, not far from Alexandria. It seemed only a matter of hours before the Nazi hordes would be at the Nile. I recall how stunned I was by the sense of fatalism with which Cairo's two million citizens were prepared to welcome the German Fascists. In their fatalism, this was just another episode in their torpid, impoverished existence. Fortunately, Rommel was beaten back by Montgomery within a few miles of the city's gates.

At its peak period, shortly before the Sinai campaign of 1956, the Suez Canal had seen the passage of some six thousand vessels a year, or nearly twenty a day in both directions. The crossover point for northbound and southbound convoys in this cut through the sand is in the Bitter Lakes, where one line of vessels must wait for the other to pass. Since June 1967, fifteen vessels have been trapped here and stand immobile in the sludge of the canal.

In the Anglo-French Suez War and Israel's Sinai campaign of 1956, Nasser sank a series of ships in the waterway to block it. Prior to this, the majority of the transiting ships were British, with a growing number of oil tankers flying the "flags of convenience" of Liberia and Panama. Soviet ships were comparatively few in number, and passage of a Russian warship through the Suez Canal was a rare front-page story.

The blocking of the canal in 1956 came as a jolt to the countries of Europe, who suddenly realized how dependent their economies were upon the oil received via this narrow waterway. No less dependent were the oil companies operating in Saudi Arabia and Iran, which shipped the black gold either through pipelines from Arab countries or in tankers built to pass through the Suez Canal. For the Arab oil countries, the shutdown also meant a stupendous loss of revenue. The lesson was not long in being learned, and a solution was soon found.

If tankers of sufficient size could be built, price comparisons showed that it would cost less per ton to ship Mideast oil to Europe round the Cape of Good Hope than in smaller tankers through the Suez. Plans were speedily drawn up and keels laid for the first of the "giant supertankers," at that time of some 200,000 tons dead weight each. Since then, 312,000-ton giants have come into use, and construction of 400,000-tonners was begun in Japanese shipyards. In this way shipping costs of oil shipments to European countries have already been reduced to half.

Following the Suez conflict in 1956, the canal was speedily cleared of its sunken hulks by an international consortium organized by the United Nations, but traffic since then never regained its pre-1956 level.

To Israel, the closing and reopening of the Suez Canal in 1957 meant nothing, since her ships and cargoes had been barred from its waters ever since the establishment of the State in 1948. In 1951 Israel appealed to the United Nations Security Council against this breach of the Israeli-Egyptian Armistice Agreement, and the Council instructed Egypt "to terminate the restrictions on the passage of international commercial shipping and goods through the Suez Canal wherever bound." But the world community failed to insist on Egypt's compliance, although this injunction was mandatory, as are all resolutions of the Security Council, unlike those of the United Nations General Assembly, which are only recommendations.

When the issue was again brought before the Security Council, the demand on Egypt to lift its anti-Israel measures was vetoed by the Soviet Union. In 1954, the Egyptians confiscated an Israel ship—the *Bat Galim*—trying to transit the canal, but the United Nations Council failed to act. In the early months of 1956, the Soviet Union again vetoed a Security Council resolution calling for free and open passage of this waterway. When the World Bank loaned Nasser the funds in 1960 to widen and deepen the canal, here was another opportunity to ensure the right of all nations to free passage. But nothing was done, and Israel was still denied the rights to which she was entitled and which all other nations enjoyed.

Israel had been persuaded to withdraw her forces from the Sinai peninsula after the 1956 Sinai campaign largely on the basis of certain "assumptions" contained in a statement by President Eisenhower. On February 20, 1957, in an address to the American people, he had said:

> Egypt, by accepting the six principles adopted by the Security Council last October in relation to the Suez Canal, bound itself to free and open transit through the Canal without discrimination, and to the principle that the operation of the Canal should be insulated from the politics of any country.
>
> We should not assume that, if Israel withdraws, Egypt will prevent Israeli shipping from using the Suez Canal or the Gulf of Aqaba. If, unhappily, Egypt does hereafter violate the Armistice Agreement or other international obligations, then *this should be dealt with firmly by the society of nations* [italics mine].

"Should be . . ." But it wasn't. Nasser never released his blockade of the canal to Israeli ships. And on May 23, 1967, he reimposed the blockade of the Straits of Tiran, after United Nations Secretary General U Thant, with unseemly haste, had acceded to his demand for the withdrawal of the United Nations Emergency Force—the final impetus for the Six-Day War.

In the years since the 1967 war, during which the canal has remained closed, a previous deeply held myth has been exploded—that without the canal, Europe would be stranded economically. We have seen the paralyzing effect in 1956 of the canal closure to France, Britain, and the other European countries. The 1967 stoppage, however, caused only temporary hardship. Well over half of the canal traffic were oil shipments, and the supertankers were ready for the round-the-Cape journey—at half the cost. Dry cargoes also could be rerouted without major dislocation, and containerized shipments were bringing shipping costs down throughout the world.

An alternative route for both oil and dry cargoes offered through Israel cannot, of course, replace the canal. But the recently opened 42-inch pipeline from Elath, pumping oil from supertankers in the Red Sea to supertankers in the Mediterranean, forms an "insurance policy" against the dangers of Arab economic blackmail to European nations. The "land bridge" across the Negeb ensures a right of way for dry cargoes also.

Egypt's prestige and economy suffer most from the paralysis of the unused waterway. Before June 1967, Egypt's income from the canal was estimated at $550,000 a day, or $200 million a year. This loss is now being made up by the oil-rich countries of Saudi Arabia and Kuwait. But the Egyptian leader paid a heavy political price for these semi-annual handouts from those two countries. He was forced to tone down and completely backtrack on his former policy of attacking the two oil moguls who called the political tune, however discordant it sounded in Cairo. Moreover, the silent ditch was a blow to Nasser's prestige as the leading figure of the Arab world. His efforts to break the impasse by heavy shelling of Israeli positions across the canal, his declared "end to the cease-fire," and the opening of the "war of attrition" against Israel failed to budge it from its entrenched position at the Suez.

And yet, the country hardest hit by the blockage of the Suez Canal is the Soviet Union. To the Russians, who have amassed a modern army and missile force twenty miles within Egypt, the Suez Canal is even more important than the Panama Canal is to the United States.

Before June 1967, the Suez Canal saw a steady stream of Russian and East European cargo ships trading on the north-south route from Russia's Black Sea ports via the Mediterranean to eastern Africa and southeastern Asia. Much of this traffic was war matériel bound for North Vietnam, as the Suez was the main channel for the Soviet Union's continuing aid to that country. Doubtless, there are many Soviet factories in the Far Eastern parts of Russia far nearer to the Vietnam front, but their production is stockpiled for eventual use against China. Soviet supplies to clients throughout the world and for the armies of their allies at war come from factories in European Russia. And the Suez Canal is the artery through which those supplies once traveled until the Six-Day War.

The factories in European Russia are still producing matériel for North Vietnam, but since June 1967 the heavily laden vessels have had to take the long route from the Black Sea via the Mediterranean, through the Straits of Gibraltar, down the shores of western Africa and round the Cape of Good Hope before turning eastwards, adding the burden and cost of thousands of miles and weeks of sailing.

The blockade of the Suez Canal is of greater significance, however, to Russian long-range strategy than it is to the military aid that Russia extends to its clients and friends. Fully aware of Great Britain's intention to withdraw the last remnants of its military and naval presence east of Suez within the coming year, Moscow is intent on moving in to take her position. With the canal open, a buildup of Soviet naval vessels in the Red Sea, Persian Gulf, and Indian Ocean would be merely a matter of a few days. Russian warships could be detached quickly from the Mediterranean squadron or even from home bases in the Black Sea. With the canal closed, the long route round the Cape of Good Hope must now be taken.

The extent of this problem came to light in May 1966, when Moscow decided to show the Red flag in the Persian Gulf. A Soviet cruiser and two escorts were detached from the Far East Fleet and had to sail halfway round the world to pay a brief call at the Iraqi port of Umm Qasr. Since then, however, the Soviet Navy has obtained the use of facilities there and a base at the Yemeni Red Sea port of Hodeida and has become a permanent feature of the Persian Gulf and the Red Sea. But the ships there are still provided from the Far East, with no easy access to home ports.

Russia's naval strategy has at last become apparent to the planners in the Pentagon. To offset the Soviet moves and build up the defenses of America's economic interests in the Persian Gulf, the U.S. Seventh Fleet is now to be shifted from the Far East to the Indian Ocean and Persian Gulf. When the Suez Canal is finally reopened to world shipping, the units of the Soviet Mediterranean fleet which will hurry through will not find a power vacuum at the southern end, with waters devoid of representatives of the Western world. The U.S. fleet will already be there.

But even so, the Soviet Union is unrelenting in its aim to ensure the speedy reopening of the Suez Canal. This explains Russia's obsessive insistence on Israel's withdrawal from the canal. While Egypt from the beginning demanded

Israel's complete and immediate withdrawal from the whole of Sinai, the Soviet Union has, at times, mentioned a "symbolic" withdrawal of Israeli forces of a mile or so from the banks of the waterway—enough to ensure its opening with the renewed passage of Russian supplies to Vietnam and of Red Fleet warships to the Persian Gulf.

XVIII

OIL
IS RICHER
THAN
BLOOD

While fighting increases in an undeclared war largely localized around the Suez Canal, one issue transcends all others in the area. Put bluntly, what really draws nations throughout the world like a magnet toward the Middle East is its wealth of oil. Beside it, other issues are incidental. Acutely aware that the very lifeblood of the Arab countries flows from their oil fields and that Arabian oil is essential for Europe's economy, the Russians have made no secret of their aims to get at this jugular vein of both the Arab oil-rich nations and their Western customers. Compared with the growing Soviet-American struggle for control of Middle East oil, the Arab-Israeli conflict is a mere sideshow.

Even without the Arab-Israeli conflict, it is a safe conclusion that the Kremlin's reach for oil would alone have propelled it into an unrelenting drive toward this single and most important resource in the region.

Not far from Mecca, a monotonous bone-dry desert which had lain dormant for centuries had been transformed in two decades into one of the most valuable pieces of real estate in the entire world. Under the sands, nature had released the gift of an ocean of black gold. American and British oil magnates gradually developed partnerships with the sheiks of Saudi Arabia and Kuwait, who moved their residences from itinerant tents to palaces from which they now travel by jet planes and specially built Cadillacs.

Saudi Arabia after 1940 was the most dramatic beneficiary of the revolutionary impact of the oil discovery on any primitive desert country. Nowhere in the Middle East has the discovery of oil produced such striking contrasts between the indigenous nomadic mode of life and the Western technological innovations introduced by the oil companies. In none of the Middle Eastern countries has the change been so radical and so artificially superimposed as in Kuwait and Saudi Arabia, and nowhere does it still seem to be so rootless.

This flow of oil from under the sands of each of the poor desert nations had the effect of springing some leaks into the framework of their political structures. The discovery of oil in Algeria in 1950 brought the revolution against the French to a boil, strengthened the Algerian revolt, and hastened De Gaulle's final capitulation to the insurrectionists. Nasser and the Russians were later disclosed to have contributed important support to the success of the rebels.

In 1955, the massive oil strike in Libya converted one of the world's poorest nations from bare rocks into untold wealth and unquestionably triggered the overthrow of King Idris by a group of young revolutionaries.

The Soviet Union, the world's second largest producer of oil, does not need Middle East oil today. While Russia is an oil-exporting nation and at present produces an oversupply, this does not mean that its long-range needs for tomorrow are assured. Some analysts say that Soviet resources have been overstated. There are also indications that some recent oil discoveries in the Soviet Union, such as that at Tyumen in West Siberia, are proving extremely costly to develop.

According to some observers, including Soviet and eastern European experts, the Soviet Union's demand for oil will, in 1980, exceed domestic supply by about one hundred million tons a year, an amount equal to half the conservative target figure for the whole Tyumen field in Siberia.

Russian engineers are already producing a trickle of oil from the bleak desert hills in northeastern Syria near the town of Karasuk. Syria plans a production rate of about thirty-six million barrels a year in this area.

In Iraq, the state-owned National Oil Company, nationalized from Anglo-Dutch interests, is opening large areas of the country to Soviet oil-exploration teams. The Soviets take oil in repayment for their assistance if the venture proves productive. The Russians are also building a steel mill in Iran in return for natural gas that will be piped from Iran into the remote Asiatic regions of the USSR. It is also known that the USSR also has its hand in developing the oil production of Algeria.

Russia's determination to obtain Middle East oil is linked with the Soviet desire to play a dominating role in the eastern European energy markets during the next few years. Concern about such domination has already prompted the eastern European countries to make their own limited but independent arrangements with the Middle East oil producers.

As might be expected, Romania was the first to take this independent step by concluding a barter deal with Iran in 1965. Since then, there have been numerous other arrangements with various producer states in which Bulgaria, Czechoslovakia, Poland, Hungary, and Yugoslavia have all been involved.

Some oil already is being wrung out of the sandy furnace of Egypt's Western Desert, where the British and Germans fought during World War II, but this is a trickle compared to the production in the range of Libya's million-barrel-a-day fields, a thousand miles farther west.

When Egypt's oil fields in the Sinai Desert were overrun by the Israeli troops in 1967, the Egyptian workers fled, but the Italian technicians and representatives of the Italian partners remained on the job to protect the installations from damage. Under Israeli direction, the oil fields were immediately put to work again.

It is understood that the government of Israel has continued to pay into a bank account of the Italian partners the same percentage of oil royalties that was paid to them by the Egyptians. Israel's present income from the Sinai oil fields helps to cover the costs of its occupation of the entire Sinai area.

The Soviet push for oil poses a sharp challenge to United States companies in the Persian Gulf area, where the oil companies have major holdings in Kuwait, Saudi Arabia, the Trucial states, Iran, Iraq, Qatar, and the Bahrain Islands.

If the Soviet Union could achieve political control over the Middle East and northern African oil-producing nations, it could hold an economic veto power over those areas of the world and their customers in western Europe and Japan, for whom Middle Eastern oil is vital.

The Russian program is to gain increasing influence in the Middle East, where some sixty-two per cent of the "free world" reserves lie beneath the sand. The areas that need Middle Eastern oil are Japan and most of western Europe. The Middle East and North Africa, with seventy-six per cent of the known "free-world" oil reserves, supply eighty-six per cent of Japan's oil imports and seventy-six per cent of western Europe's.

Until recently, deals by the Western powers with oil landlords were made with the medium of money; today, it is arms. The announcement in January 1970 of the sale of 120 French Mirage jet planes to Libya* by the Pompidou regime caused worldwide political vibrations. This followed an attempt by De Gaulle in 1968 to sell planes and rockets to Iraq worth $160 million. The arms were to be traded for oil concessions, but that transaction fell through. The Russians offered the Iraqis a better arms deal.

President Pompidou's lame reaction to the accusations that France was upsetting the arms balance in the Middle East, created as a façade by De Gaulle to woo the Arabs into a courtship of arms for oil, was that he "did not want Soviet power to filter westward."† The planes are obviously destined for Egyptian use against Israel.

---

* It is known that in all Libya there is not a single aviator with the technical training to operate one jet plane, let alone the one hundred on order scheduled to be delivered in 1971.

† Nasser's agents made no secret that they had helped engineer the Libyan deal behind the scenes with the French. According to press reports, some of the "Libyan" negotiators were actually Egyptian.

Hardly a month passes that one does not see new volatile ingredients added to the already boiling concoction of politics, power, and money that make up the oil business in the overheated Middle East.

Algeria, in early 1970, nationalized properties of four foreign oil companies—the Phillips Petroleum Company, a member of the Royal Dutch Shell group of companies, a West German company, and an Italian company.

Iraq, which had previously nationalized its own oil resources (which had been found and developed by the West), supported the Algerian move, and urged all Arab oil-producing countries to co-operate to form a front against "international oil cartels."

Libya ordered a joint venture of Texaco, Inc., and the Standard Oil Company of California to cut back production. This followed a similar command to the Occidental Petroleum Corporation.

Libya blocked the loading of two special tankers built by the Standard Oil Company of New Jersey to export liquified natural gas from Libya to Italy and Spain.

Anti-Western revolutions in the Middle East have been followed by nationalization of oil and of other Western major investments. Nasser's appropriation of the Suez Canal was a signal for the nationalization of oil in Iraq, Algeria, and Libya. It is not too difficult to foresee that Russian-inspired insurgency will one day be exported to Saudi Arabia and Kuwait.

American oilmen are still concentrating on today's profits, which blinds them to tomorrow's threat from the Soviets moving nearer and nearer. Their attempts to "buy off" the Arabs by giving way to every blackmail threat only reveals to both the Soviets and the Arabs that the oilmen are running scared. The oilmen don't know their own strength. Instead of diluting the enormous power flowing from their oil, they should put their propaganda apparatus to work in Washington to impress on the United States policy makers their obligation to protect the immense American investments by standing up to Soviet penetration.

The Soviets are in the early stages of succeeding in a subtle form of petroleum blackmail that could isolate the United States from the rest of the world, as part of the Soviet aim to outflank the United States in terms of control of world energy sources.

The Russian game of petroleum blackmail is to wean the NATO allies and the Japanese away from the United States. The Kremlin hopes to convince these governments and people that the energy which drives their economies is dependent on Soviet goodwill rather than on the activities of their Western allies, so that one day the United States will find itself isolated.

The one bit of recent good news for American and Western oil interests was the discovery of a potential giant oil field in the North Sea (off the coast of England), giving Europe for the first time a major indigenous supply of crude oil. Some estimates have placed the find at one billion tons of oil, or more than four times the present known total European reserves.

It should be noted, however, that like the north slope of Alaska, the North Sea oil find, although large, does not change the rules of the international oil game. These fields are good cards for Western Europe and the United States to have in their hands, but the Arab nations still hold all the trumps.

Western Europe is at present consuming about 560 million tons of oil a year, and thus the one billion tons could supply the area for a year and a half. The Alaskan north-slope find would supply only two years of the United States demand, if it were the only source (and if the announced figures are true, which is doubtful).

Nasser had adopted the terrorists' line in attempting to use the smear of oil in his propaganda, threatening to oust the American companies from the Middle East and deprive them of more than two billion dollars a year in oil profits.

Along with Iraq, Syria, Jordan, and the Sudan, he issued a communiqué on February 9, 1970, threatening Western oil interests for the first time since the Khartoum meeting in 1967, when the Arab leaders decided that no matter what, oil money had to continue to flow into their coffers.

The terrorists continue to gamble on the hope that the threat in itself will be enough to frighten Washington. They prefer not to face the fact that every Arab oil-producing leader knows so well: their production and oil royalties would evaporate overnight without United States major investments in the costly machinery to extract the oil from the sands and to ship and market it throughout the world.

In their revolt against Arab governments, as well as in their terrorism against Israel, the guerrillas have not hesitated to use oil as a weapon by puncturing pipelines and spilling tons of the black gold into rivers of waste and setting it aflame.

On May 30, 1969, a six-man squad of the leftist Popular Front for the Liberation of Palestine (PFLP) blew up a section of the Trans-Arabian Pipeline (TAPline) in the Golan Heights, blocking the flow of oil for the first time since the 1967 war. About eight thousand tons of oil spilled, some almost down to the Sea of Galilee. But most of it became a blazing river that Israeli soldiers and civilians fought five hours to extinguish. When the line was again cut at the beginning of 1970, the Syrians announced that they would not permit its repair. The line remains inoperative.

TAPline is owned by ARAMCO, which pays Saudi Arabia, Jordan, Syria, and Lebanon $30 million a year in transit fees. The pipeline carried 440,000 barrels of oil a day —about one sixth of Saudi production—across twenty-five miles of Israeli-held land in the Golan Heights. Saudi Arabia can ship the oil by supertankers to Europe. The losers are Syria and Lebanon, which have stopped collecting transit charges.

Egypt and Saudi Arabia both condemned the 1969 sabotage as hurtful to Arab interests and a violation of the 1967 Khartoum agreement to continue the flow of oil to the West. Cairo's newspaper *Al Ahram* denounced it as a "senseless hysteria," while Radio Jeddah in Saudi Arabia accused the terrorists of a "foreign Communist conspiracy."

The Popular Front commandos who carried out the sabotage explained that they wanted to remind the United States of the price for supporting Israel and to "punish" the Nixon Administration for "plotting" against the Arabs.

Politics and terrorism now threaten to disrupt the flow of oil under the sands. With the poverty deepening and population multiplying in Arab countries, oil is valued above human life—richer than blood. Politics may be said to be "dirty pool," but not when the pool is petroleum.

RUSSIA
CHALLENGES
THE UNITED
STATES

MIDEAST—
PIVOT
OF POWER

After a recent visit to the Middle East, I met in Washington with former associates in the Department of State and put the question squarely. "What are we doing about stopping the Russians from taking over the Middle East?" With disarming frankness the reply was: "How would *you* go about stopping them? Have *you* any ideas?"

While I could certainly offer no pat formula, I did say I could suggest some things *not* to do: for instance, *not* to employ a policy of appeasement which would build up another Munich in the Middle East; not to reach Yaltalike agreements with Kremlin leaders in attempting to foist an artificial "settlement" on the area which will explode in our faces.

"We seem to be running on quicksand, combining the worst pitfalls of both Munich and Yalta," I said, "while the bear is trudging ahead unimpeded."

Israel and other small countries, haunted by the specter of disaster from a 1970 variation of the 1938 Munich debacle of "peace in our time," are gun-shy of the game of power brokerage being played to decide their fate. They cannot forget that the losing card the British played against Czechoslovakia was the trick that turned into the cataclysm of World War II. The dirty word "Munich" came to be a synonym for appeasement.

Yet, the United States is earning for itself the opprobrium of appeasement by its maneuvers with moribund and decadent Arab regimes. Combined with a passive response to Russian machinations in the region, it reflects a retreat from political realities. Instead of blowing hot and cold, we should be blowing a trumpet of peace.

We cannot afford to sacrifice our friends in the region, while continuing to woo weak neutrals and adversaries. The military postures of these friends—Iran, Israel, Turkey, and Lebanon (aside from the shaky Arab monarchies)—and economic structures must be fortified against Soviet encroachment. Instead of holding firm for the only solution—a real peace in the area—the United States' zigzag policy and surrender to pressure from the Kremlin on the one side and to the Arabs on the other could doom the region to continued conflict.

The United States friendships with all countries must be measured exclusively in terms of American national self-interest, *and nothing else.* Within this policy, it is altogether possible that the United States needs its Middle East friends as much or more than they need the United States. American weariness from the Vietnam involvement and its shift toward isolationism cannot absolve it from its responsibility to protect its rightful position in the Middle East. Moscow is succeeding in ousting the United States as the dominant power in the Middle East. Its victory has come about not only by invitation of the Arabs, but by default of the United States. At stake is not only control of the entire Middle East, but the door of the southern ports, the Adriatic, and then to southern Europe, and the gateway to the Persian Gulf and the Far East.

RUSSIAN
WEAKNESS

It is a traumatic experience for an American on diplomatic errands to watch the United States, from the vantage point of Arab capitals, playing a losing part on the Middle East stage, but it has been my own experience. We have sat back like impotent spectators in a rapidly changing world arena while the Soviets were gradually moving into a position of dominance from which they can wedge their way into becoming the major political factor in the Middle East as well as in Europe.

For the first time in history the United States is being pushed into playing a defensive, secondary role in a region where she had inherited from Great Britain a position of dominance. If this backward step were in some area of the globe that was not pivotal and crucial for democratic governments and peace, it would not be too self-defeating. But almost as if its eyes were shut, Washington has been permitting its friends to be caught in a Russian bear-hug squeeze in an area that controls our position between the East and West.

The fallacy of this United States *status-quo* role is nakedly exposed as Russia moved swiftly to plant itself even more solidly in the area. While the United States cautioned its diplomatic missions in the Middle East capitals to take a passive role ("low silhouette" was the popular phrase last year) and became immobilized by a paralyzing war in Vietnam, the Russians moved *steadily,* and not even *stealthily,* into the Middle East. Today, the question is no longer whether the Soviet Union will reach strategic parity with the United States. They have already reached it.

This is not to say that the Russians will now move in rapidly from the Mediterranean or the Aegean Sea to capture or explode western Europe from their new vantage point. Russia's practical policy is to win in her own good time without the cost of open warfare, and to keep the area in tumult while she screws her way in by any means, fair or foul.

Internal ferment in the Arab world has been a *precondition* for the Soviet Union to become an ideal ally. The rising radical restless elements in each of the Arab countries were lured by the more eloquent promises of the Russians. What had the Americans to offer, if anything? What could the Americans bid?

Claims that the Soviet Union is merely acting in behalf of its Arab clients to defend them against Israel are a useful cover for Russia's historic strategic purposes. The Soviet imperialists hope to maintain a twilight zone of no war/no peace in the Middle East—a policy which will go to any lengths *short of all-out war* to further their aims by preventing a peace in the Middle East, other than one on their own terms. If peace were finally to be reached, and Arab interests were to turn from war to peaceful reconstruction and development at home, their dependence on Moscow would be lessened, and the possibilities for peaceful aid from the United States and the West would become an actuality.

The establishment of Israel, for which both the United States and the USSR voted in 1947, has become a historical act of good fortune for the United States and a stumbling block to Russia's later aims. A handmade democracy with the proven capability of building its own society after our image would, as a practical matter, seek our friendship. Yet, it is altogether possible that the United States needs Israel's friendship today as much as Israel needs the United States. For the little democracy stands between Egypt and Syria and next to Lebanon and Jordan, blocking Russo-Arab expansion to control the entire Middle East door to the central Mediterranean, the Adriatic, and southern Europe, the Saudi Arabian and Persian oilfields, and the road to the Far East.

If the United States will stand firm in its own national self-interest against Soviet manipulation of anti-Western "revolutionary" Arab governments, American interests will be safeguarded. If the stance of the United States weakens, Western interests, including the immense United States oil investments, will be grabbed by Arab revolutionaries and their Kremlin backers. The lesson of Libya ought to be etched in our memories.

Apart from Lebanon, with its growing Moslem majority, Israel is the only real democracy in the entire area. It is, moreover, a Western-oriented democracy that has stood up firmly against Soviet policies and threats. It has also repeatedly shown that in the face of perils, the Israelis can defend themselves without asking for soldiers from other lands. This fits neatly into the policy statements of President Nixon that the United States should undertake no further commitments of men in foreign areas. All that Israel has requested from the United States is permission to *purchase*, as she always has done, the fighter aircraft and other military equipment needed to counter-balance the massive flow of Soviet arms to Egypt and Syria. Actually, Israel should really be grateful for her enemies. Without them she could not have shown her mettle nor have gained the new ground for her security.

The irony is that the Soviet is operating from weakness and the United States from strength in the Middle East— from the strength of its latent power and the impetus of the Soviet setback in the 1967 war. For the Six-Day War was an unmitigated disaster for the Soviets, even though they are now turning it into a political victory. In the June 1967 fighting, its clients, Egypt and Syria, and their Soviet arsenal suffered a crushing defeat, and the Kremlin had been unwilling to come to their aid, fearing confrontation with the United States.

The vaunted umbrella of Russian power had failed, and the Soviets proved to be both unreliable and static. This passive Soviet performance in the crunch was lamentably ignored by United States propaganda and was forgotten by the Arabs. On the other hand, the Six-Day War constituted a substantial and *unearned* victory for the United States position in the Middle East versus the Soviet Union, which we have squandered. Israel defeated not an Arab but a Soviet-Arab attempt to strangle the tiny democracy in order to immobilize and dissolve the blockade Israel represents to the Kremlin's southward drive.

As for the United States, it emerged stronger than before—
so strong, in fact, that the blackmail of an attempted Arab
embargo on oil shipments to the West had to be rescinded
within a week. The Soviet Union, on the other hand, finding itself in a seriously weakened position, set out systemat-
ically to scuttle Israel's position and recoup its losses by political means, as well as economic and military aid to Egypt
and Syria.

Moscow hoped to bluff Washington just as it had successfully done in 1956, during the Sinai campaign. By identifying
the USSR with Arab aims, giving the Arabs the most
sophisticated modern weapons (better weapons than they
give North Vietnam and their eastern European satellites),
encouraging the Arabs to abrogate the United Nations cease-
fire, and raising the threat of an imminent war, the Soviets
hope to scare the United States into doing the job for them
that they were unable to do themselves—namely, to pressure
Israel to return to the pre-June 1967 borders. All this was
to be done under the guise of a "political solution"—which,
as used by Soviet-Arab diplomacy, has nothing to do with
peace. It is merely a euphemism for continuation of the unstable and explosive conditions which preceded the war.

As unbelievable as it may seem, the United States
swallowed the bait. Both President Nixon and Secretary of
State Rogers fell for Moscow's 1969 line of a Mideast
"powder keg" in danger of a momentary explosion. In
agreeing to accept Russia as a participant in Four-Power
talks, the United States undercut its own best interest. Israel's
bargaining position was diminished and the chance for real
peace postponed. By 1970 the area had indeed become a
powder keg packed with Soviet missiles and pilots.

Only after the Cambodian invasion was out of the way did

President Nixon appear to wake up belatedly to the Russo-Egyptian violation of the truce and the peril we faced in the Middle East.

First came the Russian fishing fleet in the Mediterranean, jam-packed with electronic gear, while modern weapons flowed into Egypt. Then came submarines, followed by the Red Mediterranean squadron. More recently, the Soviet presence in Egypt has been escalated by some 15,000 men; Russian pilots were stationed on operational duty in Egypt. By mid-1970, Soviet SAM-2 and SAM-3 missiles were set up in Egypt and along the Suez Canal, in a Mideast version of the Cuban missile scenario.

How could the Russian proposals be anything but one-sided to serve the Russo-Arab aims? Even with the participation of Britain and France guaranteed, the talks were heavily weighted in Russia's favor. Paris sided with Moscow, while the British continued to talk platitudes. The United States, by continuing the two-power and four-power talks, is handing the Soviet Union a gratuitous victory. While achieving none of its own objectives—true peace, stability in the region, and restored respect for United States influence there and throughout the world—these talks provided the Soviet Union with a façade to advance their arms shipments and military preparations in the area.

A handful of sortsighted professional Arabists, supported by some bankers and oilmen, apparently convinced the United States policy makers that their short-term business interests are identical with the national long-term good. The result is that the United States may end up by punishing its friends and rewarding its enemies—risking the ultimate loss of its oil profits and sowing the seeds of another war. There is still time for the United States not to be taken in by the

Soviet game, which is to hand the Kremlin a victory on the Potomac that it had lost on the Suez.

RUSSIAN
SMOKE SCREEN
VERSUS
AMERICAN
STRENGTH

The Kremlin is using the conflict between the Arabs and the Israelis as a smoke screen to hide its own aims in the Middle East.

The Suez is the testing ground to determine whether the flames of the Arab-Israeli semiwar will spread into a major conflagration between the United States and the USSR. The fighting over the Suez has not been with Egyptian and Israeli aircraft, but with Western against Russian fighter planes. The Russians have managed to conceal the appearance of their involvement by keeping their military observers in places where they will not fall into Israel's hands. In the autumn of 1970, their operators were exposed in bringing their missiles twelve miles from the Suez line during the declared ninety-day truce.

The air waves over the Middle East are today filled with the Russian language from Russian fighter pilots, pilots of cargo planes ferrying in missiles at the rate of one every fifteen minutes. The coded Russian communications continue apace between the "advisors" down to battalion level in the Egyptian army and the Russian soldiers who are in complete and sole control of Russia's newest missiles.

With Israeli troops on the Suez eastern bank, the Russians feel frustrated, for Israel has made it clear that it will not shrink from a clash with Soviet pilots over the Suez, if engaged by them. It is up to the United States to deter the Russians from a dangerous escalation that may end up in an East-West confrontation. In defending their positions, the Israelis have been taking *punishment* on the battlefield from Russian equipment, while the Soviets are pressing the Americans on the political front to *punish* the Israelis for their 1967 victory.

In less than fifteen years, the Russians have been instrumental in helping break American alliances and to take under their control the populations of more than 80,000,000 Arabs in Egypt, Sudan, Algeria, Syria, Libya, Iraq, and Yemen. The remaining of the United States friends in the region are in Saudia Arabia, Lebanon, Turkey, Iran, Israel, and Jordan—countries with a combined population of around 74,000,000.

While these are mere statistics, the figures serve to demonstrate the increasing power potential that the Soviet is rapidly building up as a Russian rampart against the West. Obviously, if not stopped, it will become an insuperable wall for the United States to surmount, and its momentum will sweep the Middle East into an impregnable Soviet-Red Crescent.

Our crowning success in foreign policy since the end of World War II has centered on keeping communism from overcoming Europe and Asia. The map of Europe would have quite a different orientation today if American firm policy with NATO and the Marshall Plan had not stopped Stalin cold in his drive into Europe in 1946, which inaugurated the Cold War. Stalin's gangsterism dressed in the ideological garb of Communism was on the way to take over Iran, Greece, Turkey, Italy, and possibly France.

But the United States drew a line beyond which Russia would not be permitted to go. More important, we let them know it. Czechoslovakia just managed to get under Stalin's wire in 1946, and there he was stopped.

But in the one area that is the turnstile between East and West, the Middle East, where we had inherited England's dominant position, we failed to draw that line. The Russians, sensitive to every hestitant and weak American stance, quickly moved in under the Arab tents. In so doing, we let our guard *down* and the Communists *in*.

The Russians knew precisely what they wanted. With Asia and Africa too close to their home-ground for comfort, they have a clean-cut policy to protect their borders and to drive for expansion into the Mediterranean and thence north to Europe and east and south to Asia and Africa.

To cope with this, American policy has been passive, befuddled, and unrealistic. I have read too many reports in American embassies and discussed enough policies on the Middle East in Washington to observe how well-meaning American ambassadors, cultivated and trained in dealing with peoples in other parts of the world, simply do not understand Arab psychology.

In one of my first reports to the Department of State, I said, "You can't *buy* an Arab, you can only *rent* him." The United States still feebly attempts to find common denominators in dealing with feudal Arab leaders whose ethical standards differ from our own. The Israelis, who have lived among them and speak their language, understand the Arabs and deal with them as they are. In fact, Israeli intelligence officers, members of a secret service acknowledged to be among the best in the world, have been accepted as close confidants of certain Arab leaders—an impossibility for anyone who does not understand the Arab language, life, and thought processes.

The Russians, pragmatic and tough without a trace of naïveté or sentiment in their make-up, play the game according to their own ground rules, exploit the Arabs, foment opposition to the West, use them for all they are worth, and make sure not to trust them any farther than they can throw the Kremlin.

A recent example is the United States' rejection (until the fall of 1970) of Israel's request to purchase additional Phantom planes in the naïve hope of winning more credits for America from the Arabs. In a single chorus, as if rehearsed in advance, the United States was attacked the very next day as an imperialist ally of Israel.

When will we learn how voracious and bottomless is the Russo-Arab appetite? Bending to their pressure is seen by them only as a sign of weakness and an invitation to demand more in the way of "bribes" in the hope of keeping them quiet; the effect is exactly the opposite.

In our own interest, United States policy makers must return to the old-fashioned American posture of firmness, the one that has worked so successfully in Europe, and the *only* one that is understood by the Russians.

My Department of State colleagues had asked for my suggestions in dealing with the Russian penetration into the Middle East. To help find some clues to an answer to their thorny question, I reverted to a scorecard of recent world history which I had drawn up, showing in two separate columns the results on the one side from firm positive action by Washington, and on the other side were the results of weakness and inaction.

The score shows that wherever and whenever we have taken a firm stance in any area of the world where America's vital interests are involved, the Russian Bear has been stopped in his tracks. Wherever we have faltered, he has advanced.

Here are the scores.

ON THE
ONE HAND

1. Immediately following World War II, President Truman acted swiftly and firmly with the Marshall Plan to meet the threat to Turkey and Greece from Soviet-inspired revolts. Result: The tide against Communism turned, and *Free World defenses in these two pivotal countries were safeguarded.*

2. In 1953, President Eisenhower swiftly released the United States' powerful airlift to counter the Soviet blockade of West Berlin: Result. *West Berlin was saved from Communist take-over.*

3. In 1958, President Eisenhower and Secretary of State Dulles unhesitatingly ordered U.S. marines to the beaches of Lebanon to meet a Moscow-Cairo threat against that country's independence: Result: *Lebanon's independence remained intact.*

4. In 1962, President Kennedy stood firm against Soviet attempts to place missiles in Cuba, ninety miles from American shores. Result: *Moscow backed down and removed the threat.*

5. During the 1967 Six-Day War President Johnson announced loud and clear over the "hot line" to Moscow where the United States stood in the Arab-Israeli conflict: Result: *The Soviet Union took the hint* and did not intervene militarily on the side of its Arab allies.

6. President Nixon acted firmly in September 1970 during the civil war in Jordan, when the Syrian and Iraqi troops threatened to assist the terrorists in overthrowing King Hussein's control of Jordan. The President personally visited the ships of the Sixth Fleet in the Mediterranean area, alerted American paratroopers from Germany and Turkey, and nodded assent when Israel advanced its armies on the northern frontiers of Jordan. Result: *The Kremlin pulled the Syrian troops back and the Iraqi army inside Jordan remained immobilized.*

ON THE
OTHER HAND

1. At the Yalta summit conference, in 1945, President Roosevelt failed to take a firm stance against Stalin: Result: *America's fluid positions were frozen into the Cold War.*

2. In the Suez crisis of 1956, the United States failed to take a firm stance and abandoned our friends: Result: *We lost to Russia and Egypt,* resurrecting Nasser.

3. In Lebanon in 1969, we failed to act when that pro-Western country was again threatened with a take-over by Soviet-equipped and Egyptian-backed guerrillas: Result: *Lebanon's future hangs in the balance.*

4. More recently, in 1969, we accepted Russia's demand

for equal negotiating status with the United States to impose a Big Power solution of the Middle East. Result: *We have facilitated Soviet dominance creeping into the area.*

The score of successes and failures points unmistakably to what we should do and to what we should avoid doing to protect United States interests throughout the world. For the Middle East, in particular, the scorecard unerringly spells out the lesson: We must make it clear to the Soviet Union that we intend *localizing* the conflict in order to *liquidate* it. Since the Israelis and Arabs have been doing the actual fighting in the Middle East, the Israelis and Arabs must discuss the terms of peace. There should indeed be four-power talks, but the powers should be Egypt, Syria, Jordan, and Israel. The Russian leaders should be reminded that they have insisted on direct talks in other areas where their vital security is threatened.

We must make it crystal-clear to Moscow that if it persists in the massive armament of its clients and in enlarging the corps of Soviet military "advisors" in Egypt and Syria, if it continues to move missiles closer to the Suez Canal to prepare for an Egyptian mass crossing, and if it persists in basing Russian pilots on operational missions in Egypt, it is courting danger of an open conflict. Furthermore, the Russians' encouragement and support of guerrilla activity and subversion against Lebanon and Jordan will explode in their faces. A "balance of arms" is a dated concept. If democracy is to be fortified for peace in the area, an *im*balance of arms in democracy's favor is called for as the surest deterrent to war, an imbalance against miscalculation based on *Arabian Nights* wishful thinking.

Israel aside, American vital interests are being increasingly threatened by Russian intervention in the Middle East. As in other areas of the world where our national interests are involved, the Kremlin must know unmistakably that we will not tolerate continued intervention there and will act firmly as we did in Cuba, Berlin, and elsewhere to protect our position in the free world.

There are two conflicts crisscrossing in the Middle East: the minor one between the Arabs and the Israelis; the major one, the Russians versus the United States. The danger is in not keeping them separated from an actual collision as well as in the minds of our people.

The limited Arab-Israeli crisis is still manageable. Even a declared war between them, if it comes, can be quickly stopped by the United Nations as it was in 1948, 1956, and 1967. But unless this is cooled by United States and Russian agreement to disengage and leave it to the junior partners to find agreement possibly through Ambassador Jarring or another expert in quiet diplomacy, it will boil over into a major East-West confrontation that will mean the opening round of World War III.

The score is clear, the course inescapable. Where we have stood firm, the Russians have stepped back. Where we have vacillated and failed to act, the Russians have moved forward.

A few more such moves, and the Soviet Empire will stretch from the North Pole to the Persian Gulf and capture the Middle East without firing a shot. The more than two-hundred-year-old dream of Peter the Great and Catherine II will have become a harsh reality, and the world will witness a Red Star over Bethlehem.